The  Lingo of Learning

The **LiNgo** of **Learning**

88 Education Terms Every Science Teacher Should Know

Alan Colburn

NSTApress®

NATIONAL SCIENCE TEACHERS ASSOCIATION

Arlington, Virginia

NATIONAL SCIENCE TEACHERS ASSOCIATION

Claire Reinburg, Director
J. Andrew Cocke, Associate Editor
Judy Cusick, Associate Editor
Betty Smith, Associate Editor

ART AND DESIGN Linda Olliver, Director
NSTA WEB Tim Weber, Webmaster
PERIODICALS PUBLISHING Shelley Carey, Director
PRINTING AND PRODUCTION Catherine Lorrain-Hale, Director
    Nguyet Tran, Assistant Production Manager
    Jack Parker, Desktop Publishing Specialist
PUBLICATIONS OPERATIONS Hank Janowsky, Manager
sciLINKS Tyson Brown, Manager
    David Anderson, Web and Development Coordinator

NATIONAL SCIENCE TEACHERS ASSOCIATION
Gerald F. Wheeler, Executive Director
David Beacom, Publisher

The Lingo of Learning: 88 Education Terms Every Science Teacher Should Know
NSTA Stock Number: PB179X
05   04   03   4   3   2   1

Library of Congress Cataloging-in-Publication Data
Colburn, Alan, 1961-
    The lingo of learning: 88 education terms every science teacher should know / by Alan Colburn.
      p. cm.
    Includes bibliographical references and index.
    ISBN 0-87355-228-8
    1. Science—Study and teaching. 2. Education—Terminology. I. Title.

    Q181.C5265 2003
    507'.1—dc21

2003011664

CONTENTS

CHAPTER 1 EDUCATIONAL OUTCOMES

CHAPTER 2 GENERAL INSTRUCTIONAL APPROACHES

CHAPTER 3 INSTRUCTIONAL MODELS

CHAPTER TEACHING TECHNIQUES

CHAPTER  ASSESSMENT

CHAPTER 6 DIVERSITY

CHAPTER LEARNING THEORIES

CHAPTER RESEARCH CONCEPTS

CHAPTER TEACHER EDUCATION

Alphabetical List of the 88 Education Terms

THE AUTHOR

Alan Colburn is an associate professor of science education at California State University–Long Beach. He earned his Ph.D. in science education from the University of Iowa. He holds an M.S. from the University of Illinois (biology), an M.A. and teaching credential from the University of Pennsylvania (education), and a bachelor's degree from Carnegie Mellon University.

He has taught high school classes in physical science, chemistry, and AP chemistry. Much as he enjoyed teaching on that level, he ultimately found working at the college level to be a better fit for his varied interests. In his current position, which he has held since 1995, he supervises student teachers and teaches courses for elementary, middle, and high school teachers, college students, and graduate students. He also spearheaded the development of a new master's program in science education. He has authored 22 publications—not including this book—and given 38 professional presentations. Five of the publications were in National Science Teachers Association journals.

THE REVIEWERS

Carol Collins
K–12 Science Consultant
Hamilton County Educational Service Center
Cincinnati, OH

Paul Jablon
Associate Professor
School of Education
Lesley University
Cambridge, MA

Mary Lightbody
National Board Certified Teacher—Early Adolescence / Science
Walnut Springs Middle School
Westerville, OH

Susan Mundry
Senior Research Associate
WestEd (Regional Educational Laboratory)
Boston, MA

Molly Weinburgh
Associate Professor of Science Education
Associate Director, Institute for Math, Science, and Technology Education
Texas Christian University
Fort Worth, TX

Preface

I am a university science educator. I spend my days communicating with other university science educators. I even married a science educator! As you might imagine, the language of professional education is commonplace to me. It sounds like gobbledygook to the rest of the world, but I'm not fazed to hear someone say, "Research supports constructivist teaching practices as a means to increase student achievement, when assessed authentically."

I know that I'm an exception to the rule, though. People hear this kind of talk and think of it as fancy language meaning little or obscuring commonsense ideas. Just between us, I've occasionally even thought this myself.

But I also know that the specialized vocabulary used by my colleagues represents important ideas. Sometimes I've felt this use of language was unfortunate because it created a virtual wall between the researchers who created new knowledge and the teacher audience for whom the work was ultimately intended. This book was born from that kind of thinking. I wanted to write something that would bridge that virtual wall, connecting those who do and don't regularly engage in what some have come to call "educational jargon."

The book that follows discusses 88 terms. It's meant to give readers an introduction to each of these ideas, providing more than a dictionary or glossary, but still something that can be read and understood quickly. The book is divided into chapters by topics, and I tried to write each chapter so that a reader could profitably read the chapter from start to finish and get an overview of a key area in science education.

I wrote the work with teachers in mind—prospective teachers in education courses, practicing teachers in workshops, all National Science Teachers Association (NSTA) members, and indeed anyone interested in better understanding professional education. I hope you find it understandable, useful, and enjoyable.

In each chapter I tried to include a few references that interested readers could turn to if they wanted to learn more about the chapter's topics. Many resources are available; I had to make decisions about what references to include. I tried to choose articles and books that would be relatively easy for readers to find. If you are reading this, then you are probably a member of NSTA, or know somebody who is. As such, I concentrated on NSTA-published resources in my suggestions for further reading—I thought they would be easier for you to find than other resources. I included many references that are available on *NSTA Pathways to the Science Standards: Resources for the Road CD-ROM.* (This CD contains copies of hundreds of articles.) Of course, many other equally good resources are also available. We live in an age where access to professional literature has never been easier.

Finally, some thanks are due. Writing a book, no matter the length, is a daunting task. Judy Cusick and the folks at NSTA Press have been very supportive throughout the process. Besides offering occasional editing and advice, my wife has also been my biggest cheerleader—seemingly happy to hear endless recitations about how many words I wrote each day. And, finally, there are my parents. My dad wrote *Physical Science Made Easy* more than 50 years ago. Somehow it seems fitting that I would write this book, which bears a few similarities, since he has been my life template in so many ways. This book is better, though—and my mother's influence has something to do with that. As she would be the first to tell you, I've come a long way since the sixth-grade report where I tried to tell readers everything there was to know about the U.S. Air Force in five pages. In the pages that follow I certainly don't try to tell you everything—just enough to get you started.

Educational Outcomes

At the beginning of the 21st century, education seems dominated by talk about educational outcomes and their assessment. This chapter, along with the chapter on assessment, serves to demystify these topics.

In truth, outcomes are easy to understand. Several related terms describe what students should learn—how they should be different at the end of a lesson, unit, or course when compared to the beginning of the instruction. Terms about outcomes simply differentiate types of learning and specificity levels—from broad outcomes down to specific "factoids."

objective The idea of an objective in education comes from the concept of the *behavioral objective*. Behavioral objectives grew out of the 20th century learning theory called *behaviorism*. One of the theory's major tenets is that the only things that can be assessed educationally are those that can be directly observed. Thus, behavioral objectives represent observable educational outcomes—what students should do.

The traditional behavioral objective, as taught to a generation of teacher education students, has three parts: (1) the things students are to be given to demonstrate their ability, (2) the expectation of what students will be able to do, and (3) how well the students are expected to perform to be considered competent. Example behavioral objectives might be "Given a periodic table, students will be able to determine the formulas for ionically bonded compounds with 80 percent accuracy" or "Given experimental data and graph paper, students will be able to construct a graph with all data plotted accurately." (In the latter example, the "all" serves as the criterion for how well students are expected to perform.)

Behavioral objectives stated this rigorously are less common today than they used to be. However, the concept is still alive and well. Objectives are statements about what students should know or be able to do, usually after a relatively brief period of instruction, such as a teacher-led lesson or the silent reading of a passage in a textbook. Because objectives help you think through what you want your students to be able to do, they're helpful as a starting point for thinking about how to teach a lesson. They're also helpful as a place to begin thinking through how you want to assess students after a lesson or unit. Ideally, the various objectives, teaching methods, and assessments should be highly congruent.

benchmarks The concept of the benchmark (or bench mark) has, of course, existed on its own for a long time. In recent times, in science education, the term has been most closely associated with *Benchmarks for Science Literacy* (AAAS 1993), a publication of the American Association for the Advancement of Science. In that publication, the authors note a dictionary's definition for "bench mark"—"a standard or point of reference in measuring or judging quality, value, etc." (317). They go on to say that their benchmarks "are offered as reference points for analyzing existing or proposed curricula in the light of science-literacy goals" (317) and that they are using the word for the goal statements in their report.

It's difficult to distinguish benchmarks from standards. To AAAS, at least, the distinction between a standard (see next entry) and a benchmark is that the benchmark is essentially a goal *statement*, whereas the standard is closer to a *measure* indicating that a learner has minimum competency in understanding or mastering the benchmark. Thus, a benchmark about students understanding the content of a science discipline might correspond to a standard of students earning some minimum score on a standardized test.

Readers must understand, however, that many people use the terms "standard" and "benchmark" synonymously. Others talk about benchmarks as being checkpoints to be assessed or mastered along the way toward mastering larger standards. Thus, when people are talking about standards and benchmarks, it may be useful for listeners to ask speakers to clarify what they mean by the two terms.

Clarification may also be needed to distinguish benchmarks from objectives. Again, people sometimes use the terms synonymously. However, objectives (or behavioral objectives) often refer to a smaller or more specific educational outcome; a benchmark could be subdivided into a number of objectives. Thus, as used by many, standards are broader than benchmarks, and benchmarks are broader than objectives.

standards At the dawn of the 21st century, the word "standard" is probably the most often heard educational term around. Everyone seems to talk about standards, often with the adjective "higher" placed before the word. With so much use, the term's meaning has become somewhat diffused. For this book, I turned to the two most important among the current national science teaching reform documents.

According to the *National Science Education Standards* (NRC 1996),

> *[t]he term "standard" has multiple meanings. Science education standards are criteria to judge quality: the quality of what students know and are able to do; the quality of the science programs that provide the opportunity for students to learn science; the quality of science teaching; the quality of the system that supports science teachers and programs; and the quality of assessment practices and policies. Science education standards provide criteria to judge progress toward a national vision of learning and teaching science....* (12)

The other major science education reform document, the American Association for the Advancement of Science's

Benchmarks for Science Literacy (1993), has a more specific definition of the term:

> *A standard, in its broadest sense, is something against which other things can be compared for the purpose of determining accuracy, estimating quantity, or judging quality. In practice, standards may take the form of re-quirements established by authority, indicators such as test scores, or oper-ating norms approved of and fostered by a profession.* (322)

The concept of a standard is closely related to other assessment concepts. Whether assessing summatively or formatively (see Chapter 5, "Assessment"), the assessor needs *something* against which to compare the "assessee's" performance. Standards represent that "something." (However, note the previous entry on benchmarks, too. People often use the terms "standards," "benchmarks," and "objectives" interchangeably. "Goals," "aims," and "outcomes" are other terms people sometimes use synonymously with those just mentioned.)

Bloom's taxonomy has its origins in the same era that brought behavioral objectives. It was established as a taxonomy of cognitive knowledge—a way to distinguish "lower-order" thinking from "higher-order" thinking. It is still a popular way to categorize knowledge and think about educational outcomes. When people talk about "higher-order thinking" they are often speaking about the three or four highest levels within Bloom's taxonomy.

Although Benjamin Bloom originally discussed other kinds of knowledge, the taxonomy that bears his name is concerned specifically with cognitive (thinking) knowledge. Bloom's taxonomy divides knowledge into six categories. From lowest to highest order, the categories are *knowledge, comprehension, application, analysis, synthesis,* and *evaluation.*

Knowledge, or rote-level knowledge, describes information that has, essentially, been memorized. The knowledge may or may not mean much of anything to the learner. Knowing that the letters Hg on a periodic table stand for mercury, that salamanders belong to the class Amphibia, or that the Greek letter μ stands for one millionth is each an example of information at the rote knowledge level of Bloom's taxonomy. Reciting a memorized definition of the term "benchmark" also represents knowledge-level understanding.

Comprehension, on the other hand, represents understanding at a slightly deeper level. It means being able to explain an idea in one's own words—rather than, say, repeating a memorized definition (which would still be knowledge-level learning). Being asked to define a benchmark in one's own words would be an example of a comprehension-level question. The idea is that using one's own words to define or explain something represents a higher level of understanding than merely

repeating a memorized definition.

Application refers to understanding something well enough to apply it to a new situation. Many educators consider this to be the true test of whether students really understand concepts. Problem solving is often application level. Making predictions about what one thinks will happen in a particular situation is also considered to require application-level understanding.

Analysis, in this case, implies the kind of understanding required to take a complex idea or issue and break it down to component parts. *Synthesis,* on the other hand, is about combining ideas to come up with new conclusions, implications, or other ideas. Finally, *evaluation* is about critically appraising a complex idea or issue—not merely saying something is "good" or "bad," but having well-thought-out justifications for the evaluation.

As an example, here are sample questions about frogs at each level of Bloom's taxonomy:

Knowledge	To which kingdom, phylum, and class do frogs belong?
Comprehension	How are frogs able to live in water (as tadpoles) and on the land (as adults)?
Application	How would you prepare an environment to grow frogs?
Analysis	How are frogs and fish alike? How are they different?

Synthesis	What could you do to find out how many frogs live around a particular lake?
Evaluation	Which of your classmates do you think had the best method to find out how many frogs live around a lake? Why do you think so?

affective domain This

phrase refers to students' attitudes, interests, and values. Generally applied to particular subject matter, or school in general, the affective domain is that part of education concerned with emotion. The affective domain is often contrasted with the cognitive domain when thinking about assessment or teaching. "Cognitive domain" (or "cognitive outcomes") refers to thinking—things such as learning facts or concepts, applying ideas to new situations, and thinking critically.

"Affective domain" (or "affective outcomes"), on the other hand, refers to things such as the extent to which students like science (or school), aspects of science students like or dislike most, thoughts about the place of science in society, and appreciation of the values of science.

Affective outcomes are quite difficult to assess meaningfully for individual students, because students will respond in ways to please their teachers. In most classrooms it wouldn't be an accurate assessment to have an exam question that read, "Do you like science? (a) yes (b) no." Students might say yes, even if they would more honestly respond no.

However, affective outcomes can be assessed honestly and accurately. Teachers can find out, for example, whether students tended to like science more at the end of a class than they did at the beginning of the class. Teachers can also use affective data to improve their instruction. For example, teachers can determine students' attitudes toward different instructional activities, such as those that are conducted in the science lab. Armed with information, teachers can tailor classes to best fit their students' attitudes.

science literacy is a

catchall term used by many educators and scientists. As such, no single definition fits perfectly. However, I think "science literacy" is best defined as the knowledge, skills, and dispositions needed by all informed citizens to function effectively in our society.

Notice that the definition includes "knowledge, skills, and dispositions." This means science literacy is not only about facts, concepts, and their application, but also about science-related skills and the affective domain (see above entry). A scientifically literate individual understands what science is and likes it, or at least appreciates it.

Note also that the definition mentions "all informed citizens." The implication here is that scientific literacy is about the science required by everyone—not just college-bound students or future scientists, for example. People can argue whether the college-bound student or prospective scientist should have a different kind of K–12 science education than others, but scientific literacy refers to science appropriate for and required by all.

REFERENCES & FURTHER INFORMATION:

Just about any science methods textbook will include discussion about various educational outcomes, as well as Bloom's taxonomy. A good place to learn more about standards, benchmarks, and other aspects of science education outcomes would be the key national documents on this topic, Project 2061's Benchmarks for Science Literacy *and the* National Science Education Standards. *Both documents are discussed in Chapter 10, and both are available online:*

American Association for the Advancement of Science (AAAS). 1993. *Benchmarks for Science Literacy.* New York: Oxford University Press. [available online at *http://www.project 2061.org/tools/benchol/bolframe.htm*]

National Research Council (NRC). 1996. *National Science Education Standards.* Washington, DC: National Academy Press. [available online at *http://search.nap.edu/html/nses/html/*]

For a shorter introduction to these documents, see:

Close, D. et al. 1996. National Standards and Benchmarks in Science Education: A Primer. *ERIC Digest.* [available online at *http://www.ed.gov/databases/ERIC_Digests/ed402156.html*]

The January 2000 issue of Science and Children *(vol. 37, no. 4) had several articles related to standards, including the following:*

Demers, C. 2000. Analyzing the standards. *Science and Children* (Jan.): 22–25.

Dillon, N. 2000. Sowing the seeds of the standards. *Science and Children* (Jan.): 18–21.

Kelly, C. A. 2000. Reaching the standards. *Science and Children* (Jan.): 30–32.

Stearns, C., and Courtney, R. 2000. Designing assessments with the standards. *Science and Children* (Jan.): 51–55.

Finally, the concept of science literacy is discussed at length in Science for All Americans, *the AAAS book that preceded Benchmarks:*

American Association for the Advancement of Science (AAAS). 1991. *Science for All Americans.* New York: Oxford University Press. [available online at *http://www.project 2061.org/tools/sfaaol/*]

General Instructional Approaches

STS, science-technology-society

Advocates of science-technology-society (STS) approaches in the United States believe that the science curriculum should pay special attention to science-based social issues. The curriculum should be personally relevant to students. STS advocates envision K–12 science classes being best when focusing on the boundary between science and society (Yager 1992).

Educators have advocated STS ideas for many years, particularly during the early 1980s (Yager 1990). In some ways, STS was a reaction to perceived short-comings in discovery- or inquiry-oriented curricula that had been popular during the preceding decades. Some people believed the National Science Foundation–funded "alphabet soup" curricula (see Chapter 10) placed too much emphasis on science classes as a way to interest the most able students in science careers. Trying to attract some students to science careers ultimately shortchanged other students, according to critics of those curricula. Society on the whole was also shortchanged, they said, because science today requires a knowledgeable public to support and monitor scientists' activities. So, STS-based approaches to the science curriculum were (and are) based around the idea that science is for all students, and should be oriented toward students' learning about relevant social and technologically based scientific issues that affect everyone.

STS-based approaches are still alive and well, in various guises. Environmental education is very much an STS-oriented curricular approach. Similarly, activities where students do things like write letters to elected officials about science issues, role-play stakeholders in a town hall meeting about a science-related issue, or care for a local pond are all STS oriented.

The current incarnation of STS curricula is often combined with a content-oriented emphasis. The result has been curricular projects like *Chemistry in the Community* (ChemCom) and *Biology: A Community Context*. These texts try to portray science in a way that is personally relevant and issue oriented, while still teaching students about the basic facts and concepts forming the basis for many state science standards.

problem-based learning is something of a combination of STS (above) and student-centered instruction (p. 11). In problem-based-learning classrooms, students are asked to create solutions to real-world problems. Like most real-world situations, the problems that students are given are often messy, with few clear-cut

answers, and the process that students follow toward solutions is group oriented (Wright 1992). Working to solve case studies is a common example of the problem-based approach, but by no means the only instructional model defining the approach. In science classes, students may even go into the field to work on real-world problems. The approach is the antithesis of classrooms where teachers act as experts, guiding students to neat solutions for contrived problems.

Problem-based learning is probably most associated with medical schools, where groups of students work together on medical cases. Case studies also frequently form the basis for instruction in law schools and business schools. Thus, the approach has filtered from professional schools to K–12 classrooms. As such, problem-based learning seems to be most common as an instructional approach among older or gifted students.

Proponents of problem-based learning posit that the approach is ideal for preparing people for professions in which they are expected to work independently, defining and solving problems without guidance from supervisors. They say the approach helps students develop critical-thinking and problem-solving skills, while learning basic science concepts. When successful, the approach is one that creates enthusiasm on the part of both teachers and students.

Critics point toward large changes asked of students and teachers, because problem-based learning is so very different from more traditional ways of teaching and learning. Students are asked to work together, often somewhat independently of their teacher. They may not (initially) know what to do and may demand clearly laid out expectations for everything they are expected to do to receive a high grade on their work. Success also requires good skills for working as part of a group.

Teachers are also asked to undergo major adjustments. Extra work must be done ahead of time in preparing the case and accompanying materials, and teachers have to learn how to assist students without directing everything they do (Good and Brophy 1992).

Still, examples do exist of commercially available and well-regarded problem-based curriculum materials. For instance, the modules in Dale Seymour Publications' *Event-Based Science* are often centered on a case study representing a real-world problem. In the *Oil Spill!* module, for example, students role-play different types of consultants working in teams to make decisions about where to locate a new port for oil tankers. Along the way, students engage in activities in which they learn about density, buoyancy, tides, and a variety of other topics.

integrated science, coordinated science

The phrase "integrated science" has dif-ferent meanings among educators. All definitions of the phrase relate to the idea of teaching students about a science discipline simultaneously with something else. Differences in definitions for the term center around two issues. The first is what the "something else" is that students are learning simultaneously with a particular science discipline. The second difference among definitions deals with the degree of integration between different subject matters (or how the integration occurs).

In defining the idea of integrated science, the first question to address is what subjects are being integrated with science. At least three broad classifications of subject matter integration exist (Davison, Miller, and Metheney 1995). First, teachers frequently integrate multiple science disciplines (biology and chemistry, for example). Second, science and a separate school subject are sometimes taught together, most commonly science and mathematics. A third classification of integration is science with multiple school subjects. Teachers often accomplish this through thematic instruction, where teachers in multiple disciplines are teaching about ideas related to a theme running through several classes. The theme may represent a particularly relevant or "real" idea. In addition, elementary teachers are often interested in integrating science instruction with reading and writing instruction.

Beyond defining *what* is to be integrated, advocates also must describe *how* the curriculum will be integrated. The adjective "integrated" usually implies more "togetherness" than "coordinated." Integrated science units teach subject areas simultaneously, whereas coordinated science units are more sequenced, with one following the other.

In recent years, coordinated science has most strongly been associated with the National Science Teachers Association's Scope, Sequence, and Coordination project (SS&C, which is described more fully in Chapter 10). SS&C's vision was one in which the traditional "layer cake" of high school science—with students learning biology, then chemistry, then physics—would be replaced by a curriculum in which students learned every science, every year. In theory, students would revisit core science ideas as they progressed through high school (or K–12). As students aged, they would learn more abstract aspects of the science curriculum's key ideas. Students might very well still take courses in biology, chemistry, and so forth—just every year, for part of the year, rather than all at once for an entire school year.

The education community finds it difficult to define "integrated science" and "coordinated science" because much integrated/coordinated science fits somewhere between the spectrum of totally integrated and totally coordinated science.

Despite vagaries in deciding *what* is to be integrated with science, and *how* it is to be integrated, proponents of integrated science agree on a few basic assumptions. The science disciplines themselves are becoming increasingly integrated (e.g., biochemistry, geophysics). Science and mathematics go hand in hand so strongly, supporters argue, that it makes sense to teach them together (of course, this idea also has its detractors). Science that is personally relevant or oriented toward real-life applications almost always draws on multiple disciplines. Finally, science is deeply integrated with important public policy issues that every citizen should understand.

thematic instruction

is a type of integrated instruction in which a general theme or idea is the centerpiece of instruction in multiple disciplines. For example, consider a middle school thematic unit about agriculture. Students learn about the importance of agriculture to developing culture in a world history class, read classic stories about farm lives in an English class, and study plant germination in a science class. The social studies, English, and science teachers work together—perhaps teaching students in a school-within-a-school setting.

Thematic instruction is most popular at the elementary school level, where classes are self-contained and the same person is likely to teach English, social studies, math, science, and other subjects to a group of students. Teachers tend to see less cross-curricular thematic instruction at upper levels because of the difficulties of coordination among classes. Still, advocates are quick to point out the advantages of this type of teaching arrangement. Science classes tend to become more application or real-world oriented, focusing on topics students find more interesting than those covered in traditional science courses—and perhaps in greater depth. English teachers like the fact that students read and write in multiple disciplines, practicing reading different types of material. Of course, students presumably learn to make connections between disciplines.

teacher-centered instruction/direct instruction

Generally put, in "teacher-centered instruction" the teacher's role is that of a knowledge expert whose major job is to pass knowledge directly to students. The student's job is to absorb or otherwise assimilate the new knowledge. Having students listen to lectures, fill out worksheets, passively watch TV or videotapes without any context or follow-up, and even (sometimes) complete a reading assignment are examples of teacher-centered instruction. In some conceptions of the learning cycle model of instruction (see "learning cycle," p. 21), teachers deliver the term or concept introduction phase of the

model via teacher-centered instruction. (Indeed, just about any time one sees instruction referred to as being "delivered" it is teacher-centered, direct instruction that is being discussed.)

The most commonly seen form of teacher-centered instruction is the lecture. The lecture remains the most enduring and practical of all teaching methods. As such, the phrase "teacher-centered instruction" is almost synonymous with lecture—even though it really refers to a variety of direct instructional methods. Direct, teacher-centered instruction occurs anytime knowledge is meant to travel directly from the teacher into the student.

student-centered instruction

Advocates of student-centered instruction think of the student as being an important participant in his or her learning. Basically, they believe that learning is a process whereby people must mentally *do* something with new knowledge before it's truly learned. People do not learn by passively absorbing new information. Research about how people learn supports this idea—indeed, it's probably the central idea guiding study about learning and thinking (cognition). I discuss this more in Chapter 7, "Learning Theories."

The student-centered-education view is reflected in John Dewey's (and others') educational philosophy, which is experience-based and subscribes to Socratic teaching methods; hands-on, minds-on learning; and indirect teaching methods. These ideas all share the thought that people learn when they interact with their environment and, simultaneously, draw upon previous life experiences. Dewey was famous for positing that a child's education should begin with the child and his or her experiences, with the curriculum as the ultimate educational goal. Similarly, people still associate Socrates as a teacher with asking open-ended questions and responding carefully to what one's students say.

Open-ended questioning, journals, and inquiry-based science lab activities all represent examples of student-centered instruction. Most educators think of the exploration and application phases of the learning cycle model as being student-centered instructional activities. In student-centered methods, the teacher's job is to set up a situation where students can successfully be guided to new learning. Students work actively to understand what's happening around themselves. In today's parlance, students "actively construct new knowledge." (For more on this concept, see "constructivism," p. 58.)

mastery learning as

we think of it today originated in the 1960s. Certain educators began challenging an assumption at the root of education—that teaching produces a range of

student learning because some students have more abilities than others. Instead, the suggestion was made that some students simply learn faster and more easily than others.

The implication of this idea was that the reason some students didn't do well was because the school didn't meet their learning needs. Given enough time and varied kinds of teaching, all students could master the entire curriculum. Ultimately, a trade-off had to be made: teaching time versus student learning. Mastery learning proponents believe student learning is more important than time factors—it's better for everyone to learn key concepts, even though it means students will progress at different rates.

It works something like this: Students are informed of a unit's objectives and then taught in ways that are supposed to help them master the objectives. They are then tested. Those scoring above some minimum are deemed to have mastered the objectives and move on to something new. Those scoring below the minimum receive additional instruction before being retested. Theoretically, the assessment-reteaching cycle continues indefinitely. In practice, of course, it does not.

Science teachers today seem to generally accept the assumptions underlying mastery learning. They also seem to recognize the trade-offs between time and student learning. This is probably mastery learning's greatest legacy.

Mastery learning approaches, however, seem to be uncommon in science classrooms. Teachers find mastery learning–based programs difficult to implement and manage. This is particularly true in schools with high student-to-teacher ratios, high rates of absenteeism, lots of students in pull-out programs, minimal instructional materials, and large numbers of students with serious or idiosyncratic difficulties that require extra teacher attention (Good and Brophy 1992).

reception learning

is probably most strongly associated with learning psychologist David Ausubel. Reception learning is, basically, the product of direct teaching. Ausubel said that learning was most meaningful when teachers helped students connect what they already knew to what we expected them to learn. He stressed that young children benefited most from hands-on activities and other kinds of direct experiences. In the higher grades, however, he advocated increased use of more direct teaching/reception learning (LeFrançois 1991).

As I mentioned in the "teacher-centered instruction/direct instruction" entry above, people sometimes think of the term "direct teaching" in the narrow sense of lectures (or lecture-like activity), even though other teaching activities can also be considered direct instruction. Similarly, there's a danger in interpreting reception learning as part of a passive

process. Ausubel always maintained that the most important factor in successful teaching and learning was that the teacher understand what his or her students already know and orient instruction toward modifying students' concepts or changing their misconceptions.

In that sense, his ideas were similar to those of today's constructivists. Reception learning, at the time it was popular, was something of a reaction or complement to ideas about discovery learning. Advocates of reception learning maintained that learning from direct, unguided experience was, at best, inefficient. To understand complex new ideas, they maintained, required that someone assist students in ways that helped them make sense of what they were learning, relating the new ideas to experiences and knowledge that the students already possessed.

In many ways, today's accepted ideas about how people learn science concepts represent something of a synthesis between the seemingly opposing ideas of reception learning and discovery learning.

discovery learning

Like many aspects of teaching, the concepts behind discovery learning are hundreds of years old. However, discovery learning became a commonly used phrase about a generation ago. It's based on a straightforward belief: The ideas we tend to retain are those we create for ourselves. We learn best when we figure things out—or discover things—for ourselves.

Proponents of discovery learning think about learning as a process of categorizing sense perceptions and ideas (LeFrançois 1991). Concepts ultimately represent new categories of information for the learner. As such, learning is a process of taking in new information and figuring out how it fits in with everything one already knows. Supporters advocate the idea that the best way to learn is by a sequence parallel to the ways we develop cognitively. The youngest of children understand and learn via direct sensory experiences. Older children (and many adults) can also learn via the introduction of literal or concrete representations of ideas. The last part of this developmental progression is the ability to abstract new ideas in more symbolic or generalizable ways.

Discovery learning had a profound impact on science instruction in the 1960s and 1970s. Some of the best-known elementary curricula from that time period were based, at least in part, on ideas consistent with discovery learning. Curriculum projects like the Elementary Science Study (ESS) and the Science Curriculum Improvement Study (SCIS) were discovery oriented. In typical activities, children would be excitedly working on open-ended exploratory lab activities, begun with a series of questions and a handful of materials provided by the teacher. Discovery was also important as underpinning for several instructional models, including the learning cycle and the various forms of inquiry-based instruction.

Criticism of discovery helped lead the way to today's constructivism-based classrooms. Many people interpreted discovery learning as being very open ended and unguided, with little or no emphasis on students' background knowledge or experiences. As applied to the classroom, teachers sometimes found discovery-based approaches to be cumbersome or, in their minds, unrealistic and unproductive.

Some of the criticisms are probably fair. Others were perhaps the result of the fast, widespread dissemination of discovery-based models and techniques—important baseline ideas were diluted or lost along the way. However, with slight modification, discovery-based ideas are alive and well today, still playing a leading role in science educators' ideas about effective science teaching.

REFERENCES & FURTHER INFORMATION:

Davison, D. M., Miller, K. W., and Metheney, D. L. 1995. What does integration of science and mathematics really mean? *School Science and Mathematics* 95(5): 226–30.

This article discusses various ways that people integrate math and science, but I think it's equally appropriate as a guide toward ways to integrate science and other disciplines. The ideas might even apply when thinking about integrating multiple science disciplines, like physics and geology.

Good, T. L., and Brophy, J. E. 1992. *Looking in Classrooms*. New York: HarperCollins College Publishers. (Newer editions available.)

This book is a good, all-around reference about teaching and research on teaching. It's comprehensive and detailed, combining scholarly support for ideas with practical suggestions.

LeFrançois, G. R. 1991. *Psychology for Teaching*. Belmont, CA: Wadsworth Publishing Co. (Newer editions available.)

This is an educational psychology textbook; I find it to be more readable—and interesting to read—than most ed. psych. textbooks.

Wright, R. G. 1992. Event-based science. *The Science Teacher* (Feb.): 22–23.

Available on NSTA Pathways to the Science Standards: Resources for the Road CD-ROM; *for information on the CD, go to* http://store.nsta.org.

Yager, R. E. 1990. STS: Thinking over the years. *The Science Teacher* (March): 52–55.

Available on NSTA Pathways to the Science Standards: Resources for the Road CD-ROM; *for information on the CD, go to* http://store.nsta.org.

Yager, R. E. 1992. Appropriate science for all. *Science Scope* (Nov./Dec.): 57–59.

Available on NSTA Pathways to the Science Standards: Resources for the Road CD-ROM; *for information on the CD, go to* http://store.nsta.org.

Instructional Models

cooperative learning

As its name implies, cooperative learning happens when individuals work together to help each other learn. Cooperative learning procedures represent teaching methods that are well supported by research (Johnson, Johnson, and Maruyama 1983; Sharan 1980; Slavin 1980).

In practice, however, readers must distinguish between *cooperative learning* and *group learning*. Group learning happens when teachers place students together in groups and provide a task to complete. If the students understand the task, are capable of completing it successfully, and work together well, then the learning that happens may be better than any student could have completed on his or her own.

However, as many teachers know, simply placing students in groups does not guarantee success for anyone. That's why cooperative learning advocates usually discuss particular criteria that need to be in place before they can truly call group learning "cooperative learning." Although details vary somewhat from advocate to advocate, most cooperative learning advocates point out four broad conditions distinguishing cooperative learning from other methods.

First, students are simultaneously interacting with each other. Although individual students are talking only to members of their group, *many* students are talking at any given moment. (This contrasts with the traditional picture of a classroom, in which only one person talks at a time.) Second, individual conversations are more or less equal. This means that one student is neither dominating the group's work nor participating to a much lesser extent than any other group member. Third, students depend on each other in order to be successful—the way members of sports teams depend on one another ("positive interdependence"). Finally, the teacher still holds everybody responsible for all the learning ("individual accountability"). Thus, most cooperative learning advocates frown on the use of group grades for anything important. The teacher still expects each student to learn everything.

One of the more popular cooperative learning techniques is called the "jigsaw." Suppose, for example, that students in a high school science class were learning about the anatomy and physiology of various animals—earthworms, frogs, starfish, and crabs. The teacher might divide students into groups of four. (It's beyond this book's scope to go into issues such as how to choose group members or to manage a cooperatively structured classroom. For information on such topics, see Ossont 1993; Robblee 1991; Watson 1992.) Student A in each group (there might be seven or eight groups in a class) is responsible for learning particular things about the anatomy and physiology of the earthworm. Student B is responsible for the same information applied to frogs. Student C is assigned the starfish, and student D is assigned the crab.

Then, each student meets with other students in the class who are learning about the same animal—for example, the student As from each group become part of a new, temporary group to learn about earthworms. These students meet as a team of specialists, gathering information, doing lab activities, becoming experts about their animal, and rehearsing their presentations.

Eventually, all students return to their original groups and are responsible for teaching their peers about the anatomy and physiology of their animal. In this case, the peer's teaching should be more or less an application of information each student learned about his or her animal. Student B, who learned about respiration in frogs, would get a lesson from Student A about respiration in earthworms. Although Student B learns, it's important to note that Student A also learns—having to teach others is a valuable way for the *teacher* to learn (as a lot of teacher-readers will confirm when asked about their first few years in the classroom!).

The teacher then tests students on what they have learned about animal anatomy and physiology from their fellow group members. Remember, everybody in the class ultimately learns about the anatomy and physiology of *all* four animals.

Successful teachers often teach using short, highly structured cooperative learning activities until they are certain their students have the necessary abilities and knowledge to work together productively. The teacher may also initially spend time teaching students particular social skills they need to work together successfully. These skills can range from simpler things—such as speaking in a voice loud enough for the group to hear without disturbing the rest of the class—all the way to complex skills—such as learning how to disagree with others while still respecting their viewpoints. These initial investments pay off later; students are more skilled at working together, and groups have fewer conflicts than they would without this training time. Indeed, some teachers even like cooperative learning more as a means toward teaching students the value of these kinds of social skills than for other educational goals.

inquiry, inquiry-based instruction

Historically, discussions of inquiry generally have fallen within two broad classes. Sometimes people talk about inquiry as describing what scientists do and sometimes as a teaching and learning process. Authors of the *National Science Education Standards* (NRC 1996) seemed to recognize this dichotomy:

> *Scientific inquiry refers to the diverse ways in which scientists study the natural world and propose explanations based on the evidence derived from their work. Inquiry also refers to the activities of students in which they develop knowledge and understanding of scientific ideas, as well as an understanding of how scientists study the natural world. [emphasis added] (23)*

To make this distinction less confusing, people also sometimes use the phrase "inquiry-based instruction." This term refers to the creation of a classroom where students are engaged in (essentially) open-ended, student-centered, hands-on activities. This means that students must make at least some decisions about what they are doing and what their work means—thinking along the way.

While most people in the science education community would probably think of inquiry as hands-on, it's also true that many educators would "count" as inquiry any activity where students are analyzing real-life data—even if the information were simply given to students on paper, without any hands-on activity on their part.

As readers can begin to see, inquiry and inquiry-based instruction represent ideas with broad definitions and occasional disagreements about their meaning. Two people advocating inquiry-based instruction may not be advocating for the same methods! Some define "inquiry" (instruction) in terms of open-ended, hands-on instruction; others define "inquiry" in terms of formally teaching students inquiry skills (trying to teach students how to observe or make hypoth-

eses, for example); and some define inquiry so broadly as to represent any hands-on activity (see "verification activities," p. 21).

Another area some science teachers disagree about relates to the feasibility of inquiry-based instruction for all students. Those not supporting inquiry often portray the teaching methods as appropriate only for advanced or gifted students, saying that some students lack requisite background information or thinking abilities to be successful in an inquiry-based atmosphere. Inquiry supporters often counter with examples of inquiry-based instruction seen in elementary school classrooms. Well-known examples include the open-ended ESS (Elementary Science Study) curriculum as well as the learning-cycle-based SCIS (Science Curriculum Improvement Study) materials. More recent examples include FOSS (Full Option Science System) and the National Science Resource Center's STC (Science and Technology for Children) curricula.

structured inquiry activity
In a structured inquiry activity, the teacher gives students a (usually) hands-on problem they are to investigate, and the methods and materials to use for the investigation, but not expected outcomes. Students are to discover a relationship and generalize from data collected.

The main difference between a structured inquiry activity and verification lab (or "cookbook activity") lies in what students do with the data they generate. In structured inquiry activities, students are largely responsible for figuring out what the data might mean—that is, they analyze and interpret the data. Students may ultimately interpret the data differently; different students may come to somewhat different conclusions. In a verification lab, on the other hand, all students are expected to arrive at the same conclusion—there's a definite right answer that students are supposed to be finding during the lab activity.

A sample structured inquiry activity might be the classic physical science activity in which students find relationships between the length of a simple pendulum and its period (assuming students are familiar with these concepts). In this activity, the teacher (or lab manual) would tell students they are to find the relationship between a pendulum's length and period and would provide necessary materials and directions to follow to answer the question. It would be up to the students, however, to both figure out the data they need to record and interpret the data's meaning.

guided inquiry activity
In a guided inquiry activity, the teacher gives students only the problem to investigate (and the ma-

terials to use for the investigation). Students must figure out how to answer the investigation's question and then generalize from the data collected. Authors have also used the phrase "extended discretion" to describe this type of activity.

For the pendulum example discussed under "structured inquiry activity," a guided inquiry version would include everything in that example, except that students would also have to figure out a procedure to follow to address the question. Presumably, some variation would exist among the procedures that students follow.

open inquiry

activity Open inquiry, in many ways, is analogous to doing science. Problem-based learning and science fair activities are often open inquiry experiences for students. Basically, in an open inquiry activity students must figure out pretty much everything. They determine questions to investigate, procedures to address their questions, data to generate, and what the data mean.

Although not strictly open inquiry with this definition, the pendulum example discussed in "structured inquiry activity" and "guided inquiry activity" would approach open inquiry if the teacher simply told students to "investigate pendulum behavior" or "figure out factors that affect a pendulum's period,"

using whatever materials students deemed appropriate. Presumably, various students would ultimately be performing a wide variety of investigations.

verification

activities, sometimes called "cookbook activities," are hands-on science lab activities that provide students with step-by-step directions for the procedures teachers expect them to perform, as well as information about the data to collect. Leading questions or statements help students successfully pay attention to the observations desired by the activity's writers. A cookbook activity is basically the same thing as directions for students to use to complete a demonstration.

In the pendulum example I've used throughout this chapter, a verification activity version of the lab would be one in which the teacher (or lab manual) tells students what they will be investigating, lists the necessary materials, gives detailed directions about what to do, and provides data tables or other ways to help ensure that students record the desired information about the pendulum's period as its length and weight changed.

learning cycle The learn-

ing cycle model of instruction traces its roots back to the Science Curriculum Improvement Study (SCIS) of the early 1960s. SCIS was one of the post-*Sputnik* "alphabet soup" curricula (these are curricula of that time period, generally produced with federal funding, that are commonly known by their acronyms—see Chapter 10, "Documents"). Few instructional models in science teaching have such combined strength in terms of both research support and theoretical support (Abraham 1997). Theoretical support comes from the model's connections to both Piagetian ideas and constructivist theory (ideas discussed in Chapter 7, "Learning Theories").

Different versions of the learning cycle exist today. However, the general pattern is to begin instruction with students engaged in an activity designed to provide experience with a new idea. The idea behind this exploratory phase of the cycle is that learning of new ideas is maximized when students have had relevant, concrete experience with an idea before being formally introduced to it (Barman and Kotar 1989).

This exploratory phase is ideally followed by a concept- or term-introduction phase. That phase generally begins with class discussion about student findings and thoughts following the previous part of the cycle. Sometimes the teacher can then go on to simply provide names for ideas that students previously discovered or experienced.

Finally, students expand on the idea in an application phase of instruction in which they use the new idea(s) in a different context. Using a new idea in a new context is an important part of maximizing learning. In addition, some students don't begin to truly understand an idea until they've had the time to work with it for a while, in different ways. The learning cycle model provides these students with time and opportunities that help them learn.

Ideally, the application phase of the cycle also introduces students to a new idea. In this sense, the application phase of one learning cycle is also the exploratory phase of another learning cycle—hence the "cycle" part of "learning cycle." (Notice that the previous sentence began with the word "ideally"; sometimes it's difficult for an application phase activity to also encourage students to explore other ideas.)

The classic batteries and bulbs series of activities represent an excellent example of a learning cycle. In the exploratory phase of the cycle, students are asked to figure out ways to make a bulb light, given only a battery, length of wire, and lightbulb. Students explore multiple ways to get the bulb to light, arrived at by manipulating the battery's poles and the lightbulb's arrangement with the wire and battery.

Students come to see that they need to create a loop going from one end of a battery, through the piece of wire, through the lightbulb, and back to the battery (usually with some part of the bulb touching an end of the battery). This is the perfect time to formally introduce students to the concept of an electrical circuit (concept- or term-introduction phase). Students have already experienced the idea, so the teacher only needs to provide a name and formal definition to something students can already discuss in their own words.

Students then try to find ways to make multiple bulbs light. In this sense they are using the concept of an electrical circuit in a new context (application phase), while simultaneously exploring another concept (series and/or parallel electrical circuits).

Learning cycle advocates would be quick to point out that this is a bare-bones description of the model and that what happens before, during, and after each phase of the cycle is important for maximizing student learning. Still, the learning cycle and its variations constitute probably the most widely accepted instructional model within the science education community. (For more information on the learning cycle, the reader might want to refer to an article I wrote with a colleague a few years ago [Colburn and Clough 1997].)

5E model

The 5E model of instruction is a variation on the learning cycle model, pioneered by the Biological Sciences Curriculum Study (BSCS 1993). The five Es of the model are *engage, explore, explain, elaborate*, and *evaluate*. *Engage* refers to beginning instruction with something that both catches students'

attention and helps them relate what is to come with what they already know. *Explore* is virtually identical with the exploration phase of the learning cycle (discussed above), as *explain* is the concept- or term-introduction phase and *elaborate* is the application phase. *Evaluation* is both formative and summative (see Chapter 5, "Assessment"), since it helps determine whether instruction should continue or whether students need more time and teaching to learn the unit's key points.

REFERENCES & FURTHER INFORMATION:

Many references related to cooperative learning are available. I list the following three articles because of their quality and also because they are available on a CD: NSTA Pathways to the Science Standards: Resources for the Road; *for information on the CD, go to* http://store.nsta.org.

Ossont, D. 1993. How I use cooperative learning. *Science Scope* (May): 28–31.

Robblee, K. M. 1991. Cooperative chemistry. *The Science Teacher* (Jan.): 20–23.

Watson, S. B. 1992. Cooperative methods. *Science and Children* (Feb.): 30–31.

I also believe that Spencer Kagan's cooperative learning "structures" provide a good basis for teachers interested in starting to teach with cooperative learning ideas. You can find information about Kagan Publishing & Professional Development's books and workshops online at http://www.kaganonline.com.

For a more exhaustive look at the research base supporting cooperative learning, I recommend the following three lengthy articles from the Review of Educational Research, a journal published by the American Educational Research Association (AERA) and likely to be available at most universities that have education faculty. The authors are well-known for their contributions to the research literature on the topic.

Johnson, D. W., Johnson, R., and Maruyama, G. 1983. Interdependence and interpersonal attraction among heterogeneous and homogeneous individuals: A theoretical formulation and a meta-analysis of the research. *Review of Educational Research* 53: 5–54.

Sharan, S. 1980. Cooperative learning in small groups: Recent methods and effects on achievement, attitudes, and ethnic relations. *Review of Educational Research* 50: 241–71.

Slavin, R. E. 1980. Cooperative learning. *Review of Educational Research* 50: 315–42.

To better understand the ideas behind inquiry-based instruction, especially different types of inquiry (structured inquiry, guided inquiry, etc.), see:

Colburn, A. 2000. A primer on inquiry. *Science Scope* (March): 42–44.

Martin-Hansen, L. 2002. Defining inquiry. *The Science Teacher* (Feb.): 34–37.

For an accessible introduction to the learning cycle, I recommend the following:

Barman, C. R., and Kotar, M. 1989. The learning cycle. *Science and Children* (April): 30–32.

In addition, Michael Clough and I wrote an article to help teachers move smoothly from more traditional ways of teaching toward ways that are closer to the learning cycle idea:

Colburn, A., and Clough, M. P. 1997. Implementing the learning cycle. *The Science Teacher* (May): 30–33.

If you wish to better understand the theoretical foundations of the learning cycle and the research supporting its use, I suggest:

Abraham, M. 1997. *The Learning Cycle Approach to Science Instruction.* [available online at *http://www.educ.sfu.ca/narstsite/publications/research/cycle.htm*]

Other references cited in this chapter:

Biological Sciences Curriculum Study (BSCS). 1993. *Developing Biological Literacy.* Dubuque, IA: Kendall/Hunt.

National Research Council (NRC). 1996. *National Science Education Standards.* Washington, DC: National Academy Press. [available online at *http://books.nap.edu/html/nses/html/index.html*]

Teaching Techniques

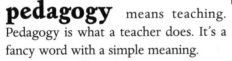

pedagogy means teaching. Pedagogy is what a teacher does. It's a fancy word with a simple meaning.

Sometimes, pedagogy is contrasted with curriculum, with "curriculum" referring to *what* is taught and "pedagogy" referring to *how* the curriculum is taught. Thus, the lecture method would be a pedagogical reference and the textbook a curricular reference. In reality, the distinction between pedagogy and curriculum can be a bit difficult because what is taught and how it is taught are deeply intertwined. As a general definition, though, pedagogy remains synonymous with teaching. In fact, if I'd wanted to I could have called this chapter "Pedagogical Techniques"!

advance organizer

An advance organizer's purpose is to provide a link between things students already know and ideas they are expected to learn in a new lesson. Grounded in educational psychology, advance organizers are presented at the beginning of lessons to help students make those connections. Advance organizers also help students organize the new material. Definitions, analogies, and generalizations can all be advance organizers (Eggen, Kauchak, and Harder 1979).

Although we usually associate advance organizers with cognitive information—facts, generalizations, and the kinds of things that can be taught via methods like lectures—I experienced a good advance organizer many years ago at a first-aid class. The class began with a videotape in which actors portrayed people in situations where knowledge of first aid would be helpful—for example, someone having a heart attack, another person choking, and another needing mouth-to-mouth resuscitation. Because these were real-life situations that we could relate to, the vignettes were a powerful introduction to the value of knowing first-aid procedures.

The class continued with students learning the procedures. Each procedure was demonstrated on videotape. The demonstration was the same scene students saw at the beginning of the course. Thus, for example, when we were taught how to stop someone from choking, we first re-watched the vignette we'd seen in the advance organizer. This combination of videotapes served to link together parts of the course into a unified whole (at the same time that they helped class members link the skills they were learning to familiar situations).

Teachers can make use of the same kind of thinking by beginning a class with a real-life example whose understanding forms part of the basis of the lesson to come. For example, consider a biology class where students are to learn about the cell cycle—the general process of how cells divide and what the cells look like at various points throughout the process. If the teacher feels comfortable mentioning cancer to his or her students, this topic

could represent an advance organizer for the lesson. Most people have at least some familiarity with cancer; it's clearly a real-life topic. Cancer, on the cellular level, is uncontrolled cell growth. Cells continue to divide under conditions in which they would normally have stopped. To understand cell division, and the kinds of strategies scientists use when trying to figure out how to stop cells from dividing, requires understanding the cell cycle. Thus, a brief introduction to cancer as uncontrolled cell growth helps provide students with a rationale for understanding an idea they might otherwise see as esoteric (the cell cycle) and helps them to link the learning to come with ideas they already understand. This kind of linking is required for meaningful learning.

On the other hand, advance organizers can also be simpler. Another advance organizer example would be a teacher beginning a lesson by simply helping students understand how the content to follow fits with things they have previously learned. "Yesterday you learned about _____; today you will learn about _____. The connection between the two ideas is _____, and these ideas fit into our unit as a whole because _____."

Advance organizers are supported by research (Lott 1983) and experience, as well as the well-understood idea that meaningful learning requires learners to link what they are learning to what they already know.

anticipatory set

This term comes from Madeline Hunter's "elements of lesson design," a concept that has been popular in many school districts and universities throughout the last 25 years. Hunter's model has both its advocates (Hunter 1991) and detractors (Berg and Clough 1991). Generally speaking, the Hunter model is based around a teaching cycle that involves setting a goal, practicing a new skill, receiving feedback, practicing further (independently), and being evaluated.

The "anticipatory set" is usually the first of Hunter's lesson design elements. The purpose of the anticipatory set (sometimes called the "focusing event") is to focus students' attention on a lesson's topic or goal, before the lesson begins. In the language of Hunter's elements, the anticipatory set focuses students' attention on the lesson's objectives. It's the way the lesson starts. Anticipatory sets are also part of transitions between parts of a lesson. When something new starts, the teacher once again needs to focus students' attention, via another anticipatory set.

Examples of anticipatory sets students might commonly see include the teacher providing a handout to students about the day's lesson when they enter the classroom, review questions written on the blackboard (designed to link yesterday's class with today's—thus also acting as a simple advance organizer), or problems displayed on an overhead that the teacher expects students to solve.

A good anticipatory set will not only focus students' attention, but do so in a way that really captures their interest and whets their appetites for what is to come. Thus, discrepant events (see entry below) are excellent anticipatory sets. Unexpected results focus students' attention in a way that leaves them asking, "Why did this happen?" Similarly, a demonstration or other way to directly connect the lesson to come with real-world applications or events is another good anticipatory set. Questions, stories, role-plays, simulations, news stories, even jokes can all be anticipatory sets.

discrepant event

A discrepant event has an unexpected outcome. Discrepant events are surprising, puzzling, or even astonishing. They are motivating (Shrigley 1987). Here are some classic examples from the physical sciences. The teacher takes two identical ice cubes and drops them in individual glasses of "water." (In one of the glasses, the "water" is actually alcohol; any kind of alcohol will work.) In one case the ice cube floats, but in the other case the ice cube sinks. Or, perhaps the teacher takes a glass, fills it with water, places a 3" x 5" card over the glass, and inverts the card/glass combination. Contrary to students' expectations, the card stays attached to the glass. Finally, you might be surprised to learn that an orange will float, but an orange *without* its peel—which, of course, is lighter than its unpeeled counterpart—will sink. These are all discrepant events. They don't appear to follow basic, everyday rules for how things are "supposed" to behave. That's what makes them so motivating. After any good discrepant event, an observer will wonder, "How does that work?"

Teachers capitalize on this curiosity and use discrepant events in various ways. They're often used by teachers as demonstrations followed by discussion, as ways to engage students in inquiry and critical thinking, as lab activities, or as challenges for students to begin investigations. In the words of cognitive psychologists, discrepant events initiate disequilibrium and begin the process of cognitive change. In the words of everybody else, discrepant events throw off our thinking a bit, because the results are so different from what we expected. We automatically begin wondering what's going on and feel motivated to better understand.

By the way, discrepant events differ from magic, even though they sometimes look like magic tricks. Magic is meant to be astonishing and entertaining. Certainly, discrepant events have the same effects. However, discrepant events have additional purposes. They demonstrate science principles, and teachers design the events to lead to student thinking or even investigations. The value of a discrepant event comes not only from the surprising outcome during a demonstration, but also from the classroom activity that *follows* the event itself.

graphic organizers

are visual ways that help students understand and process new learning. Graphic organizers are particularly beneficial, of course, for visually oriented students. Many different types of graphic organizers exist, including a host of examples used by elementary teachers and those teaching students who are learning English. However, since this book focuses on middle and high school science teaching, I will restrict my discussion to three graphic organizers commonly used by secondary science teachers—concept maps, vee maps, and KWL charts.

concept maps are diagrams meant to show how someone understands a particular topic or idea. Concept maps are branched diagrams, usually arranged from general to specific ideas. Concepts are circled, lines connect them, and words are added to show connections between the various concepts. See the sample concept map on p. 29.

Concept maps, as envisioned by Novak and Gowin (1984), are tied to David Ausubel's learning theory (see "reception learning," p. 13). Meaningful learning, Ausubel said, happens when learners relate new concepts to their pre-existing cognitive structures, which means basically all the ideas and relationships between the ideas that a learner already knows and believes. Seen this way, a concept map is almost a visual repre-

Concept Map on the Topic "Soil"

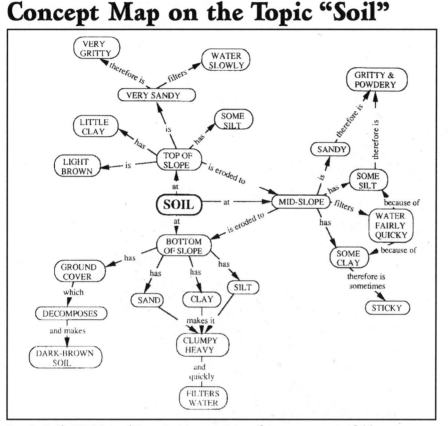

Source: Roth, W.-M., and Bowen, M. 1993. Maps for more meaningful learning. *Science Scope* (Jan.): 24–25.

sentation of a little piece of a person's cognitive structure. As such, concept maps are a good way to get a sense of how students understand scientific ideas, especially overarching or "big" ideas. Misconceptions often show up on concept maps.

Concept maps are also a good way to help students see connections between ideas. As a high school teacher I often accompanied lectures by drawing a concept map, adding concepts and links as I introduced them. This technique had the added advantage of helping to organize my presentations, ensuring that I'd never introduce ideas without having already discussed something to which I could link the new ideas.

Dorough and Rye (1997) provide a guide to the mechanics of making a concept map. Although not a step-by-step procedure—everyone makes concept maps differently—the authors do break the process down into general steps. First, list the concepts you think are most important for understanding the concept map's central topic. Second, group the concepts. You'll probably group similar ideas together, from the general to the specific. Teachers often find it beneficial to place concepts (words) on cards, slips of scrap paper, or self-adhesive notes so that they can easily be moved around. Next, begin linking concepts together. When concepts are linked together, it's important to add words showing the relationship between the linked concepts. These linking words are usually simple words or phrases, such as "are," "can be," or "are part of." Finally, you cross-link other relevant relationships—often drawing lines going halfway around the original map!

Dorough and Rye's article also discusses scoring concept maps. This is a worthwhile point to consider, because scores generally act as an incentive for students. Learning to make a good concept map is a skill that takes practice. Students may need this incentive to make their first concept maps. With a little practice, perhaps first working on familiar ideas (rather than concepts from a textbook, for example), students quickly figure out how to make the maps. These concept maps, in turn, give the teacher a window into how students understand key ideas and often make plain students' misconceptions.

vee maps are graphical ways to help students better understand why they are doing lab activities and how scientists generate new knowledge in the lab. Vee maps help students think about what they already know before they start an investigation; the maps also direct student attention to the questions, procedures, data, and data interpretations that should be part of any successful lab activity (Roth and Verechaka 1993).

As you can see in the samples on pages 31 and 32, vee maps have two sides. One side is about what students know, and the other is about what they are doing. Throughout an investigation, the two sides continually interact with one another. What we know affects what we do, and vice versa.

Vee maps usually begin with students writing about what they already know or believe about a topic and then coming up with a focusing question upon which their investigation will be built. This question may come from the teacher (see "structured inquiry activity," p. 20) or individual students (see "guided inquiry activity," p. 20, or "open inquiry activity," p. 21). Once an investigation's focusing question is set, students are ready to start thinking about how to set up the experiment, what they need to do to answer the focusing question, and the kind of data they need to collect. Whether this information is provided in a lab manual or students figure it out for themselves, it's summarized in the vee map. The teacher

The Basic Structure of a Vee Map

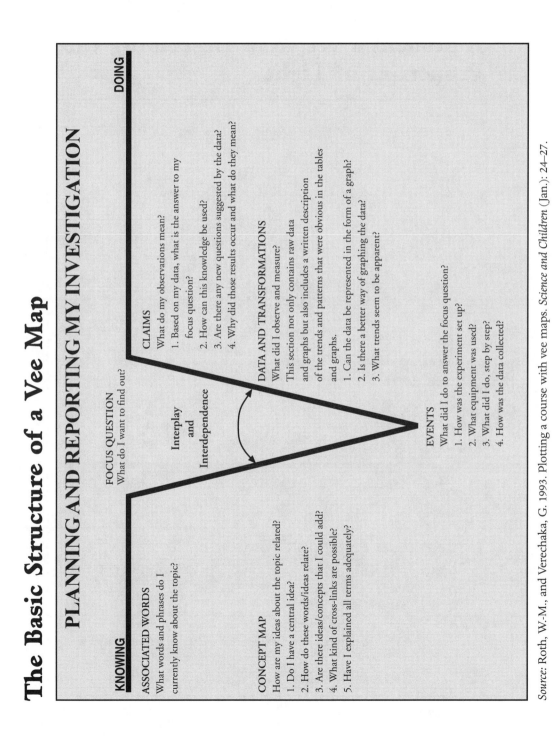

PLANNING AND REPORTING MY INVESTIGATION

KNOWING   **DOING**

FOCUS QUESTION
What do I want to find out?

Interplay
and
Interdependence

ASSOCIATED WORDS
What words and phrases do I currently know about the topic?

CONCEPT MAP
How are my ideas about the topic related?
1. Do I have a central idea?
2. How do these words/ideas relate?
3. Are there ideas/concepts that I could add?
4. What kind of cross-links are possible?
5. Have I explained all terms adequately?

CLAIMS
What do my observations mean?
1. Based on my data, what is the answer to my focus question?
2. How can this knowledge be used?
3. Are there any new questions suggested by the data?
4. Why did those results occur and what do they mean?

DATA AND TRANSFORMATIONS
What did I observe and measure?
This section not only contains raw data and graphs but also includes a written description of the trends and patterns that were obvious in the tables and graphs.
1. Can the data be represented in the form of a graph?
2. Is there a better way of graphing the data?
3. What trends seem to be apparent?

EVENTS
What did I do to answer the focus question?
1. How was the experiment set up?
2. What equipment was used?
3. What did I do, step by step?
4. How was the data collected?

Source: Roth, W.-M., and Verechaka, G. 1993. Plotting a course with vee maps. *Science and Children* (Jan.): 24–27.

A Student's Vee Map Describing the Properties of Light

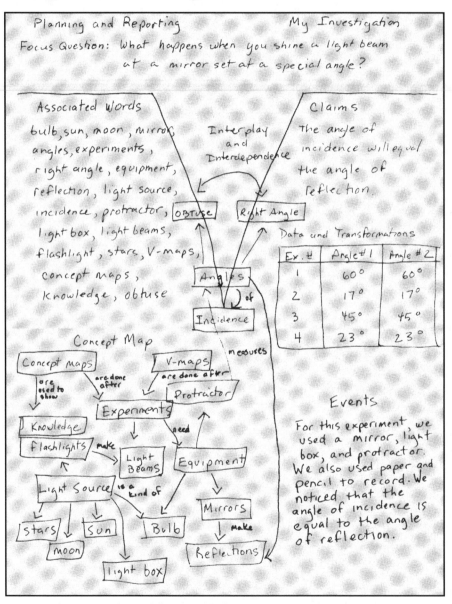

Source: Roth, W.-M., and Verechaka, G. 1993. Plotting a course with vee maps. *Science and Children* (Jan.): 24–27.

initially helps students understand how parts of the vee diagram interact with one another, and, over time, students come to better understand these interactions for themselves.

KWL charts represent a
strategy teachers use to help students better understand what they are learning. When making KWL charts, teachers lead activities that ask students to think about (or write) what they *know* (K) about a topic, to decide what they *want* (W) to know about the topic, and to monitor what they have *learned* (L) about the topic. The KWL idea builds on the concept that people learn better when they access what they already know—the "K" part of the strategy—and connect new ideas to previously learned ones—the "L" part. The strategy also helps students learn to set a purpose when they read unfamiliar text or get involved in classroom activities—the "W" part. KWL advocates note that the technique's advantages derive from its use as a metacognitive strategy. This means it helps students learn to think about their thinking—about what they already know and how this influences their current learning.

Teachers often make use of this strategy before a reading assignment or a new unit. Typically, teachers lead a classroom discussion in which students brainstorm what they already know about the topic to come. Teachers may collect responses on a blackboard/overhead, though they also often have students write individually on the question. Besides the advantages already mentioned, this activity can help teachers gain a better sense of the ideas students already have about the topic they are about to study. Students go on to generate a list of the things they would like to learn about the topic. Together, these activities represent the "K" and "W" parts of the strategy. The "L" part comes after the reading, activity, or unit, when students discuss what they have learned. KWL charts are among the more popular techniques teachers use to help students make sense of text and classroom activities.

convergent and divergent questions

Convergent questions have a single correct answer. They usually involve factual recall. "Who is buried in Grant's tomb?" and "What year did the War of 1812 start?" are both convergent questions. Divergent questions, on the other hand, may have multiple appropriate responses. "What do you think were some key factors leading to war in 1812?" is a divergent question.

The vast majority of questions that teachers ask students are convergent (Blosser 1991). Convergent questions are also called short-answer questions, since students can often respond to them with a word or two. Convergent questions are effective for assessing students' knowledge of facts.

Divergent—extended response—questions are heard much less often in classrooms than are convergent questions. Divergent questions are most appropriate when teachers are interested in learning what students are thinking or understanding about an idea at a deeper level. Versatile examples of divergent questions include "What are you observing?" "Tell me about what you are thinking." "What do you think would happen if ...?" and "How do you know?" (Penick, Crow, and Bonnstetter 1996).

Divergent questions coupled with increased "wait-time" (see next entry) are among the more effective tools teachers have at their disposal for increasing students' thinking in the classroom. Surprisingly, such an effective innovation costs nothing and can be employed by any teacher. What it takes is practicing asking extended-response questions enough so that their use by the teacher becomes almost automatic. I've found it quite beneficial to hold in my mind question stems that I could turn into full-fledged divergent questions, like the four examples of divergent questions I mentioned above. Having a sense of where I want students to go next in their learning also helps me come up with the next question(s) to ask.

wait-time In science education, the term "wait-time" is generally credited to Mary Budd Rowe (1974, 1996). It refers to how long teachers pause after asking a question, before they call on a

student or otherwise speak. Rowe found most teachers waited less than a second!

However, if teachers waited three to five seconds, positive things began to happen. Rowe found students more likely to speak, expressing complex thoughts and higher-order thinking skills. Classroom participation increased.

Subsequent work has borne out Rowe's findings. Simply put, students think more when given time to think. This means that wait-time is most important when teachers ask questions requiring student thought. Recall questions, such as "What year was *The Origin of Species* published?" or "In what phylum are red ants?," don't necessarily require the three to five seconds of wait-time as do questions such as "How do we distinguish insects from other animals?" Students basically do or don't know answers to the former questions. They may need to think about the latter question for a couple of seconds. (See the distinction between convergent and divergent questions in this chapter.)

Research also supports the idea that it's worth pausing after a student has responded to a teacher's question. Often called "wait-time II" to distinguish it from the initial pause (wait-time I), this second pause increases student participation and the number of ideas that students express.

Wait-time ultimately represents an effective yet extremely simple way to improve one's teaching. With most innovations, teachers are called upon to do more; wait-time asks teachers to do less! Along these lines, teachers should keep two points in mind. First, you may initially be a bit uncomfortable with the silence; if you force yourself to simply wait a few seconds, however, someone will probably respond. Second, students are not accustomed to classes being taught by teachers who wait after asking questions. Thus, those wonderful effects I noted earlier in this entry don't happen immediately. Students may initially not respond, perhaps even feeling embarrassed by the silence. If the teacher sticks with it long enough, though, students will get used to the silence and appreciate having time to think. Class participation will definitely increase.

nonverbal behaviors,

better known as body language, communicate with students almost as clearly as do the words we say, even as teachers and students may be unaware of messages being sent this way. "Nonverbals," for example, are one of the ways students decide whether their teachers are "serious" about something they are saying. Making sure actions and words are congruent makes for better teachers.

Positive nonverbals include smiling, keeping an open posture, leaning forward toward students, making eye contact, nodding while listening, and being at the same level as students when talking to them. When talking to students during a lab activity, for example, teachers may wish to sit or otherwise get down to the same level as students (if classroom conditions make this feasible).

REFERENCES & FURTHER INFORMATION:

For a debate on Madeline Hunter's elements of effective instruction see:

Berg, C. A., and Clough, M. 1991. Generic lesson design: The case against. *The Science Teacher* 58(7): 26–27, 29–31.

Hunter, M. 1991. Generic lesson design: The case for. *The Science Teacher* 58(7): 26–28.

To learn more about discrepant events:

Shrigley, R. L. 1987. Discrepant events: Why they fascinate students. *Science and Children* (May): 24–25.

To learn more about graphic organizers:

Dorough, D. K., and Rye, J. A. 1997. Mapping for understanding. *The Science Teacher* (Jan.): 37–41.

Hyerle, D. 1995–1996. Thinking maps: Seeing is understanding. *Educational Leadership* 53(Dec.–Jan.): 85–89.

Marzano, R. J., Pickering, D. J., and Pollock, J. E. 2001. *Classroom Instruction That Works.* Alexandria, VA: Association for Supervision and Curriculum Development. *(The book includes an entire chapter on "nonlinguistic representations," most of which are graphic organizers.)*

Roth, W.-M., and Bowen, M. 1993. Maps for more meaningful learning. *Science Scope* (Jan): 24–25.

Roth, W.-M., and Verechaka, G. 1993. Plotting a course with vee maps. *Science and*

Children (Jan.): 24–27. [available on *NSTA Pathways to the Science Standards: Resources for the Road CD-ROM;* for information go to *http://store.nsta.org*]

The classic book related to concept maps is probably still:

Novak, J. D., and Gowin, D. B. 1984. *Learning How to Learn.* Cambridge: Cambridge University Press.

For information about questions, wait-time, and questioning strategies:

Blosser, P. 1991. *How to Ask the Right Questions.* Washington, DC: National Science Teachers Association.

Penick, J. E., Crow, L. W., and Bonnstetter, R. J. 1996. Questions are the answer. *The Science Teacher* (Jan.): 27–29.

Rowe, M. 1974. Wait-time and rewards as instructional variables. *Journal of Research in Science Teaching* 11(2): 81–94.

Rowe, M. 1996. Science, silence and sanctions. *Science and Children* 34(1): 35–37. *(This article is a reprint of Rowe's earlier* Science and Children *article [March 1969] introducing the concept of wait-time.)*

Other references cited in this chapter:

Eggen, P. D., Kauchak, D. P., and Harder, R. J. 1979. *Strategies for Teachers: Information Processing Models in the Classroom.* Englewood Cliffs, NJ: Prentice Hall.

Lott, G. L. 1983. The effect of inquiry teaching and advance organizers upon student outcomes in science education. *Journal of Research in Science Teaching* 20(5): 437–51.

Assessment

Assessment, broadly defined, means information gathering. Grading (or evaluating) students is certainly one type of assessment. Tests, portfolios, and lab practicals are all assessment devices. However, teachers assess students in other ways. When teachers check for understanding, to determine whether or not to continue teaching about a particular idea and where to go next with instruction, they are also assessing their students. Ungraded pretests and self-tests likewise represent assessment. Any information that helps the teacher make instructional decisions is assessment.

Assessment is valuable to students as well as teachers (not to mention parents and other education stakeholders) because it helps students figure out what they do and don't understand and where they need to place their efforts to maximize learning. Assessment is also used to sort or rank students, letting them know how their performance compares to others', both for placement purposes and as a way to ensure minimum competencies in those who have passed particular tests.

formative assessment and summative assessment

"Formative assessment" is the phrase educators use when talking about assessment as information gathering for diagnostic purposes.

Many educators define formative assessment as something carried out *during* (or before) instruction, with summative assessment coming *after* instruction. Formative assessment is usually not used to assign grades.

An example of formative assessment outside the education field is the medical test. Generally speaking, medical tests are not things that people "pass" or "fail." The purpose of the test is to gather information that helps medical professionals decide the best treatment for a patient.

Formative assessment in the classroom is similar. Teachers get a sense of how individual students and entire classes are doing based on interpretations of student behaviors they constantly observe. This kind of informal formative assessment is a daily part of teachers' work (Atkin and Coffey 2003). When Foster and Heiting (1994) discussed "embedded assessment," they were talking about formative assessment. Teachers will occasionally quantify their observations through observation checklists or use pretests and practice tests. Even journal assignments—which give teachers information about how their students are understanding what's happening in class and what students' reactions are to the lessons—are formative assessments.

Summative assessment, on the other hand, occurs at the end—it "summarizes." Tests, quizzes, and even performances all represent summative assessments. We design them to evaluate what students have learned at the end of a unit or course as a result of instruction and the students' efforts.

It is important to understand that the *thing* used for assessment (such as a quiz or journal) does not determine whether the assessment is formative or summative. It's the *purpose* of the assessment that does that—how the teacher will use the information. Consider a teacher observing what students are doing during a lab. The teacher may watch his or her students as they work, getting a general sense of how they are doing, where they are having difficulties, and which students are developing an understanding of desired concepts. That process is formative assessment. Alternatively, the teacher may be watching for students to exhibit particular preordained laboratory skills, such as safety skills or proper use of a microscope. When observed, the teacher makes a note on a chart and students receive credit for having demonstrated they can perform the specific skill. That is a summative assessment.

Finally, the terms "formative assessment" and "summative assessment" need not apply only to students. Information about what a teacher is doing that helps him or her teach better is formative assessment—anything from anonymous, student-provided information to observing videotaped teaching sessions. An administrator's evaluation of a teacher's performance would be considered a summative assessment.

performance assessment, authentic assessment These closely related terms imply that students will be assessed based on their performances on

more real-life tasks than traditional paper-and-pencil tests. Such tasks can include projects, exhibitions, laboratory investigations, and public reports. The underlying idea is to test skills, dispositions, attitudes, or knowledge required for performing real-world tasks—by actually having students perform real-world tasks. In this sense, authentic assessment is extremely valid.

"Performance tasks" (the phrase educators often use to represent the things they ask students to do as part of their performance assessment) are generally application oriented, applying basic ideas to larger contexts or demonstrating complex skills. A lab practical exam in which students demonstrate they can use a microscope properly would be a performance assessment. Similarly, if a teacher took students aside during an electricity unit and asked them to show how they would connect a battery and bulbs to make parallel circuits, the teacher would also be assessing the students' ability to complete a performance task.

Other performance tasks are more complex. Completing an original scientific investigation, and writing a report about the work, is a performance task assessing students' abilities to generate investigable questions and carry out research to address the question.

Due to the complex nature of some performance tasks, most educators agree that the best way to assess this sort of work is with the aid of rubrics (grading standards; see entry below), understood by students before beginning their work. Achieving true reliability with authentic tasks (i.e., arriving at the same scores for equal quality work) can be difficult, however—both in terms of expense and time required.

The differences between performance assessment and authentic assessment are subtle—almost nonexistent. Technically, though, authentic tasks don't always need to be performances. For example, evaluating portfolios would be an example of authentic assessment that is not necessarily performance assessment.

rubrics (grading standards)

A rubric is a scoring tool that lists the criteria for a piece of work. In other words, the rubric tells students what "counts" for their grade. The rubric also communicates gradations of quality for each criteria (e.g., from excellent to poor) (Goodrich 1997).

So, a rubric for an assignment where students are designing and carrying out an independent investigation might include criteria for the question to be investigated, procedures for answering the question, data collection, data display, and discussion or conclusions. Each of those criteria would include a list of quality gradations. For example, the portion of a rubric for the criterion "question to be investigated" might look like this:

Question to be investigated:

[*Teacher checks one of four boxes.*]
Excellent ....❑
Question is clear, investigable, realistic for our classroom, likely to provide conclusions that could lead to further investigation.

Good ....❑
Question is clear, investigable, likely to lead to further investigations, but not realistic for our classroom.

Fair ....❑
Question is clear and investigable. May or may not be realistic for our classroom, but not likely to yield further investigations.

Poor ....❑
Question is unclear or not researchable.

By providing clear definitions for quality work, rubrics make teacher expectations clear and often result in better student work. Rubrics are also useful tools for student self-assessment and peer-assessment (students assessing each other's work to help spot areas that need improvement before they hand in an assignment).

holistic scoring and analytic (or criterion-based) scoring Education experts distinguish between two ways of grading via rubrics: holistic scoring and analytic scoring. Holistic scoring essentially means having one broad category for each level of student performance. A holistic rubric for an assignment in which a teacher asks students to design and carry out an experimental investigation might include something like this:

An "A" paper will be based on an investigable question, which is clearly stated; a procedure section that (a) addresses the investigation's question and (b) is described clearly enough that anyone could repeat the procedure exactly; an investigation that appropriately controls for variables and is repeated enough times to ensure accuracy....

Analytic scoring, on the other hand, divides expectations into multiple categories. Each category is assessed separately. In the example above, if the teacher assessed via analytic scoring, the rubric might include separate categories for how investigable the question is, the question's clarity, the extent to which the procedure addresses the question, the procedure's clarity, whether variables are adequately controlled, and so on. The sample portion of a rubric in the previous entry is a criterion-based rubric.

Each scheme has its advantages. Holistic scoring tends to be quite reliable. With a little training, different people are likely to rate assessment items (papers, projects, etc.) the same. In addition, the same person is likely to rate the same assessment item similarly each time she or he examines it.

Analytic scoring, on the other hand, provides students with more useful information about their performances. Simply telling a student she or he received a B on an assignment ultimately helps the student improve less than does providing more detailed feedback about the student's strengths and areas that need improvement.

portfolios

A portfolio is a container, a collection of mostly original work, with evidence of, for example, someone's skills, knowledge, and/or development. Most of the educational community would say a portfolio should also contain some type of commentary describing how and why the evidence within demonstrates the person's abilities. Thus, an educational portfolio combines evidence of effectiveness with reflection by the portfolio's creator.

We traditionally think of portfolios in terms of artists and photographers. Artists demonstrate their abilities by displaying their work. Consider the situation of a couple deciding whether or not to hire a particular wedding photographer. Most people would rather see pictures from previous weddings that the photographer had taken and read letters from previous customers (or talk to them), than, say, see the photographer's transcripts or results on short-answer quizzes taken during photography classes. The couple will be judging the photographer's performance abilities.

College faculty, and sometimes K–12

faculty too, are also assessed by means of portfolios. To keep their jobs, faculty must put together a portfolio that they believe demonstrates their abilities in the duties they have been asked to perform. The portfolios usually contain extensive commentary and as much documentation as the faculty member can provide to support his or her competence. A group of people judges the portfolio, in turn, making the high-stakes decision about faculty retention, tenure, and promotion. A portfolio is part of National Board Certification (described in Chapter 9, "Teacher Education").

Student portfolios are analogous to the two examples above. A student portfolio will have original student work, created over an extended time, showing different aspects of the student's abilities. A portfolio is a way to demonstrate student abilities that are difficult to assess otherwise, such as being able to design or conduct experiments or do project work or group work. Portfolios are also especially important as a way to show growth over time. In general, many in the education community consider portfolios to be a good way to assess students' abilities for performing real, or authentic, tasks.

To show the ability to design and conduct an experiment, for example, a student might include a portfolio entry with a lab report (if the lab report were open-ended enough to be considered an experiment) and/or journal entries she or he wrote while designing and carrying out the work. The student would also probably write a page of commentary to accompany the lab report and journal entries. This additional writing might discuss why the student believes the materials she or he has included demonstrate the ability to design and conduct an experiment—that is, why this material was chosen to be part of the portfolio.

At the same time, portfolios do have disadvantages. Assessing the portfolio itself is often a time-consuming activity for a teacher. Being, literally, a container, a portfolio often contains a lot of material evidence. Requiring much time and effort on the part of students, portfolios are often important assignments—they count for a lot toward a grade. As such, it is important that teachers do everything they can to assess portfolios fairly and accurately. True high-stakes portfolios—like those used for making decisions about teacher retention—are usually judged by multiple people, each trained in portfolio evaluation.

criterion-referenced tests and norm-referenced tests

Criterion-referenced tests are ones in which graders compare performance to preestablished criteria. If a teacher tells students that they must correctly answer at least 12 questions out of 20 to pass a quiz, then she or he is using a criterion-referenced test (or, more accurately, criterion-referenced grading). The written tests most people take to get a driver's license are an example of a criterion-referenced test. Anyone scoring above some minimum passes the test, and an individual score is not compared to anyone else's.

In theory, every person can pass the test. Some states are implementing high school graduation exams. A student must achieve some minimum score on the test to graduate from high school. This is another example of criterion-referenced testing, as is requiring teachers to achieve a minimum score on a test like the Multiple Subjects Aptitude Test (MSAT).

In norm-referenced tests, on the other hand, scores are ranked and compared to each other. If teachers grade on a true "curve"—such that they will record the top 10 percent of scores as As or the bottom 10 percent of scores will fail—then they are using norm-referenced grading. In norm-referenced tests, the fraction of students who pass the test will be the same—*regardless of how individual students perform.*

The SAT is an example of a norm-referenced test. Indeed, most standardized tests are norm-referenced. When examining a score, students will know what percentile rank they achieved—how they performed compared to other test takers. Norm-referenced tests are generally used to distinguish between people—like figuring out who goes to a gifted program or seeing how students in a particular city performed compared to students statewide. If you hear someone say, "Using norms established statewide, our students outperformed most schools," then that person is talking about results of norm-referenced assessments.

As a final way to distinguish norm- and criterion-referenced assessment, consider some of the clichés heard in education circles. When someone says, "Our students are among the top performing in the nation" or "Our school is one of the best in the state," support with data from tests would have to be norm-referenced. The students or schools are being ranked or compared to each other. Alternatively, "success for all" or "every student can achieve" implies assessment that is criterion-referenced.

REFERENCES & FURTHER INFORMATION:

As this book goes to press, assessment is a "hot" topic. As such, many fine references on assessment-related topics are currently available to interested readers. Three references on the topic that might particularly appeal to readers are:

Atkin, J. M., Black, P., and Coffey, J., eds. 2001. *Classroom Assessment and the National Science Education Standards.* Washington, DC: National Academy Press. [available online at *http://www.nap.edu/books/030906998X/html/*]

Atkin, J. M., and Coffey, J., eds. 2003. *Everyday Assessment in the Science Classroom.* Arlington, VA: NSTA Press.

Doran, R., Chan, F., Tamir, P., and Lenhardt,

C. 2002. *Science Educator's Guide to Laboratory Assessment.* Arlington, VA: NSTA Press

In addition, many assessment-related articles can be found on

NSTA Pathways to the Science Standards: Resources for the Road CD-ROM (for information on the CD, go to *http://store.nsta.org*). Most of the articles from here to the end of the chapter are on that CD.

About performance and authentic assessment:

Doran, R. L., and Hejaily, N. 1992. Hands-on evaluation: A how-to guide. *Science Scope* (March): 9–11.

Doran, R. L., Boorman, J., Chan, F., and Hejaily, N. 1992. Successful laboratory assessment. *The Science Teacher* (April): 22–27.

Doran, R. L., Boorman, J., Chan, F., and Hejaily, N. 1993. Authentic assessment. *The Science Teacher* (Sept.): 37–41.

Finson, K. D., and Beaver, J. B. 1994. Performance assessment: Getting started. *Science Scope* (Sept.): 44–49.

Foster, G. W., and Heiting, W. A. 1994. Embedded assessment. *Science and Children* (Oct.): 30–33.

Jones, M. G. 1994. Assessment potpourri. *Science and Children* (Oct.): 14–17.

Kleinhelder, J. K. 1996. Assessment matters. *Science and Children* (Jan.): 22–25.

Lebuffe, J. R. 1993. Performance assessment. *The Science Teacher* (Sept.): 46–48.

About rubrics:

Goodrich, H. 1997. Understanding rubrics. *Educational Leadership* 54(4): 14–17.

Jensen, K. 1995. Effective rubric design. *The Science Teacher* (May): 34–37.

Liu, K. 1995. Rubrics revisited. *The Science Teacher* (Oct.): 49–51.

Luft, J. 1997. Design your own rubric. *Science Scope* (Feb.): 25–27.

Nott, L., Reeve, C., and Reeve, R. 1992. Scoring rubrics: An assessment option. *Science Scope* (March): 44–45.

Smith, P. G. 1995. Reveling in rubrics. *Science Scope* (Sept.): 34–36.

About portfolios:

Bonnstetter, R. J. 1992. Where can teachers go for more information on portfolios? *Science Scope* (March): 28.

Collins, A. 1992. Portfolios: Questions for design. *Science Scope* (March): 25–27.

Logan, J. 1996. Authoring your own digital portfolio assessment. *Science Scope* (March): 48–49.

O'Neil, J. P. 1994. Roundtable: Portfolio pointers. *Science Scope* (Jan.): 32.

Diversity

T he Association for Supervision and Curriculum Development (2002) defines "diversity" in this way: "In education, discussions about diversity involve recognizing a variety of student needs including those of ethnicity, language, socioeconomic class, disabilities, and gender." This chapter helps readers understand some of the language often found in these discussions.

learning styles The con-

cept of learning style is intuitive—we all have preferences for how we learn. There are a couple of reasons it's important for teachers to understand that students have different learning styles. First, individual students tend to learn more readily some ways than others. Learning style advocates believe that research supports the idea that teaching students in ways that complement their strengths significantly improves achievement.

Second, we tend to teach in ways that complement our *own* learning styles. For example, visual learners often teach with a lot of visuals. Similarly, those who learn best in bright sunny rooms tend to teach their own students in as bright and sunny a room as possible. Learning style advocates believe that teaching that predominantly enhances one learning style benefits only some students.

People talk about all sorts of learning styles. Within the education community, though, the work of Rita and Kenneth Dunn is probably most strongly associated with learning styles (Dunn and Dunn 1978). Among other materials, Dunn and Dunn created the Learning Style Inventory, commonly administered to give individuals and their teachers a better sense of personal learning styles.

These researchers discuss at least 21 elements that influence learning, which they divide into five general categories. These categories are

- environmental factors, such as how bright a room is, its temperature, noisiness, etc.;
- emotional factors, such as how long someone will persist at a task in a single sitting, or where the learner places responsibility for his or her learning;
- sociological factors, meaning basically whether the student learns best alone, in pairs, in small groups, or with adults;
- physical factors, ranging from the time of day to how much one can move around while trying to learn;
- psychological factors, especially whether one learns best beginning with examples or details (eventually generalized) or prefers beginning with general information (supported later with examples and specifics).

The better-known learning preferences are those that involve seeing things (a visual preference), listening (an auditory preference), and moving around and/or touching things (a kinesthetic preference). Learning preferences that teachers commonly discuss include the extent to which students prefer learning by themselves or in groups and whether they learn best going from details to generalities or vice versa.

Learning style advocates would probably say that teachers should be aware of their own learning styles, recognize that students have different learning styles, and try to teach in ways that accommodate as many different learning styles as possible. As such, learning styles represent a researched area of education that supports and enhances many popular reform initiatives.

multiple intelligences

The concept of multiple intelligences is often associated with psychologist Howard Gardner (1983) and his associates at Harvard University. Gardner introduced the idea that many ways exist to be intelligent other than the single way measured in traditional IQ tests. He identified at least seven different kinds of intelligences—different ways to be smart or gifted. Campbell and Burton (1994) discuss Gardner's seven intelligences:

- Linguistic—intelligence in reading, writing, and storytelling. Successful authors and speakers are probably gifted in this area.
- Logical/mathematical—intelligence with numbers, computation, logical reasoning, sequential reasoning. Mathematicians, computer programmers, and many scientists are probably gifted in this area; for example, consider classical physicists setting up controlled experiments to determine definite

cause-effect relationships between established variables.

- Spatial—intelligence with mental or physical pictures, models, imagination. Artists would be among those expected to be gifted in this area. However, some areas of science may also depend on spatial intelligence for success. Earth scientists often use complex models, and chemists depend on spatial models to represent complex molecules.
- Musical—intelligence with rhythm, pitch, and other musical elements. Musicians, obviously, are generally gifted within this realm.
- Kinesthetic/body—intelligence with touch, gesture, and physical activity. Dancers, athletes, and others whom we tend to think of as being highly coordinated would all be considered gifted in this area. People who are particularly skilled in laboratory techniques may also be gifted in this area.
- Intrapersonal—intelligence with individual, reflective thinking. People we think of as being highly "thoughtful"—such as essayists Thoreau and Emerson and writers known for their diaries—may be gifted in this area.
- Interpersonal—intelligence involving groups, social skills, cooperation. Natural leaders, who are good at helping people get along, and people skilled in helping professions would all be considered gifted in this area.

More recently Gardner has suggested the possibility of another type of intelligence—naturalist (Gardner 1999).

Gardner points out that every person is an amalgam of different kinds of intelligences—everyone has all these abilities, just in different proportions. Science classes, though, tend to emphasize logical/mathematical and linguistic types of intelligences. Multiple intelligence supporters encourage teachers to teach in ways that tap into all the different kinds of intelligences that students bring to the classroom.

Multiple intelligence experts would also suggest that teachers—besides using traditional science instruction—make use of all sorts of methods to encourage and develop different types of intelligences in students (Thompson and MacDougall 2002). Examples of these methods include the following: extensive reading of nontextbook sources; extensive writing (for encouraging or developing linguistic intelligence); making pictures, models, or creative stories (spatial intelligence); creating music to accompany science activities or sometimes just having background music on in the classroom (musical intelligence); hands-on activities (bodily/kinesthetic intelligence); journal writing (intrapersonal intelligence); and cooperative learning (interpersonal intelligence).

Gardner's multiple intelligences have a direct, intuitive appeal to many teachers. They represent a positive way to talk about diversity, individuality, and ways that almost everyone can demonstrate his or her intelligence.

gifted and talented

For most of the last century, school officials defined giftedness in terms of a test score (e.g., a score on an IQ test) or high grades. With this kind of standard, somewhere between 1 and 5 percent of the children at a school were generally considered gifted. This criterion, however, is changing. According to the National Association for Gifted Children (NAGC) (2002), "a gifted individual is someone who shows, or has the potential for showing, an exceptional level of performance in one or more areas of expression." For example, a person may be exceptionally talented as an artist, a violinist, or a physicist. NAGC points out that federal legislation refers to gifted and talented children as those who could perform at a high level in specific academic fields or in areas such as creativity and leadership and who, to fully develop their capabilities, require services or activities not ordinarily provided by the school.

I think two points are particularly noteworthy about the latter definition of giftedness. Although the accent is on academic fields, giftedness is not defined solely in terms of school subjects or otherwise doing well in school. Educators sometimes equate being gifted and talented with an abundance of one or more of Gardner's multiple intelligences, that is, gifted athletically, talented musically, and so forth.

Also, giftedness requires services or activities not ordinarily provided in school. Put together, this means giftedness refers to something other than being smart, doing well in school, and being pleasant. As I point out to prospective teachers with whom I work, gifted students don't necessarily do well in school—think Einstein, for example—and aren't necessarily pleasant. Gifted students, of course, are sometimes very pleasant, but having an abundance of talents in one or two areas occasionally brings with it lack of social skills or talents in other areas. Gifted students cannot be stereotyped; the gifted have the same range of emotional traits and social skills as everyone.

SDAIE/sheltered instruction

SDAIE is an acronym for "Specially Designed Academic Instruction in English." For purposes of this work, I'll treat SDAIE as being synonymous with sheltered instruction. In an article I wrote with a colleague for *The Science Teacher* (Colburn and Echevarria 1999), we defined sheltered instruction this way:

In a sheltered science class, teachers use specific strategies to teach science in ways all students can understand while at the same time employ techniques that promote English language development. Some teachers see sheltered instruction as nothing more (or less) than good teaching because it incorporates many of the strategies found in high quality non-sheltered instruction. Sheltered classes, however, are distinguished by careful attention to students' needs related to learning another language. (36)

Ideally, sheltered instruction teaches students the same content they would be learning in "regular" science classes—it's not meant to be watered-down. Teachers are just more aware of how they are using English, speaking in ways that help English learners best understand, and teaching with methods to help students understand even if their English skills are still under development—using, for example, pictures, models, demonstrations, graphic organizers, and of course, hands-on laboratory activities.

Teachers can structure hands-on activities in ways to be more or less helpful to students learning English. Anything that helps students see and touch what they are to learn is helpful. At the same time, students are hindered by unfamiliar language defined in ways they don't understand. In the sample activity my co-writer and I discussed, potentially unfamiliar language included the terms "calculate," "predict," "buoyant," "ratio," "mass," and "density."

We looked at various ways teachers could let students practice using the terms by reading, writing, listening, and speaking. Students could work in pairs, in small groups, and as a whole group (fluent speakers tend to answer questions posed to the whole class much more often than nonfluent speakers). My co-writer also mentioned the importance of not just *telling* students something—for example, how they should set up their lab notebooks or how to make a graph—but also *showing* them what completed products would look like.

It's also important for teachers to keep language goals in mind (in addition to content goals) when working with students learning English—teachers want to find ways for students to *practice* using and understanding academic language. Assessment is also an issue for teachers when designing academic instruction in English. Students may understand the science ideas, yet receive low grades because they don't understand some of the words on a test or quiz.

ESL, LEP, ESOL Each

of these acronyms represents instruction for students whose first language was not English, who are now taking classes taught totally (or mostly) in English. "ESL" stands for "English as a second language"; "LEP" for "limited English proficiency"; and "ESOL" for "English for speakers of other languages." A student who is taking such instruction is sometimes referred to as an "ELL"—English language learner. The popularity of the various acronyms comes and goes. What has remained constant, though, is that United States schools enroll several millions of students born into non–English-speaking households and that those students face special challenges in the classroom. It's difficult to learn science while struggling with the subtleties of English.

Waiting until a student is fluent in English before teaching him or her science, however, is generally regarded as a poor idea by the education community. This is because it takes several years to become academically fluent in a language, and by then the student would be hopelessly behind in science. (Discussion on this issue is beyond this book's scope. Interested readers may want to read Bernhardt et al.'s 1996 article from *The Science Teacher*.)

However, I would like to distinguish between basic language fluency and academic fluency (Spurlin 1995). The distinction is important to those who work regularly with nonnative English speakers. Basic language fluency means a person can have a conversation on a wide variety of familiar topics and function well for purposes of everyday discussion (outside formal classroom settings). People can have basic language fluency while still not being academically fluent in English. Academic fluency means the student can understand the technical language taught in classrooms. Basically, a sizable difference exists between being able to talk to your neighbor about everyday topics and being able to understand the kinds of topics presented in typical high school science classes. The article I mentioned in the previous paragraph gives the example

of students trying to figure out the difference between planetary *rotation* and *revolution*. Similarly, I remember observing a class of mostly native Spanish- and Khmer-speaking students struggling to figure out what *chromosomes* and *genes* were, while trying simultaneously to learn how the terms differed.

Experienced teachers will undoubtedly look at these examples and say that native English speakers have difficulties with the same concepts. Thus, experts in the area of teaching school subjects to students learning English like to point out how teaching techniques that help English language learners also help students already fluent in the language. Such techniques include teaching students new ideas in multiple ways (or at least explaining ideas multiple times, using different kinds of words each time), demonstrating ideas, providing pictures or some kind of visual representation of new concepts, and offering direct experiences with new ideas (as one might find in hands-on science activities).

inclusion, mainstreaming
The education of children with disabilities, or special needs, is an educational issue that stirs passions among stakeholders—including parents, students, and teachers. Experts and advocates often hold strong and conflicting views on issues such as inclusion, mainstreaming, and individu-

alized educational plans. The Education for All Handicapped Children Act of 1975 (known to many as Public Law 94-142) mandated free and appropriate education with related services for each child—from birth through age 24—in the least restrictive environment (LRE) possible and an Individualized Education Program (IEP) for each qualifying child. Much of the controversy surrounds the phrases "least restrictive environment possible" and "free and appropriate education." The concepts of inclusion and mainstreaming describe two types of educational environments for children with special needs.

Basically, "inclusion" describes a classroom where everyone is educated together. Inclusion classes often require a special assistant to the classroom teacher. In a fully inclusive school, all the students would follow the same schedules and have equal opportunities to participate in field trips, extracurricular activities, and other school activities. Some advocates of inclusion, however, urge that academic decisions should be made on a student-by-student basis; they support partial inclusion—having some activities or learning experiences occur in alternate facilities from the classroom.

In the inclusive classroom, teachers can make all sorts of small adaptations to help students with special needs (Simons and Hepner 1992). These adaptations include using varied teaching techniques, trying different seating arrange-ments, teaching notebook organization, using transparencies (which are available after class), letting students use word processors instead of writing by hand, providing copies of notes and sample projects, allowing extra time to complete classwork, and using wait-time and special signals. Small changes in classroom activities, lab work, and testing can make a large difference to students. Simons and Hepner also note the importance of clear and frequent communication among teachers, parents, and other adults involved in students' education. The education of special needs students should be a team effort.

While "mainstreaming" also describes situations in which students with disabilities are placed into classrooms with their non-special-needs peers for part of the day, these students are also generally taught part of the school day in separate classrooms (often called resource rooms) or in off-campus sites. For mainstreaming to be most effective, teachers may need special training, students may benefit from information about their peers with special needs, and teachers, parents, and school staff should work together closely.

Of course, it should be noted that whatever the extent of adaptations required, teachers, schools, and school districts are legally mandated to educate all students appropriately—even if the teacher is not prepared to do so or the school lacks resources (Hamm 2002).

REFERENCES & FURTHER INFORMATION:

Association for Supervision and Curriculum Development (ASCD). 2002. A Lexicon of Learning: What Educators Mean When They Say...

This is an online publication at http://www.ascd.org/cms/index.cfm?TheView ID=112

Bernhardt, E., Hirsh, G., Teemant, A., and Rodriguez-Muñoz, M. 1996. Language diversity and science: Science for limited English proficiency students. *The Science Teacher* (Feb.): 25–27.

Available on NSTA Pathways to the Science Standards: Resources for the Road CD-ROM; *for information on the CD, go to* http://store.nsta.org.

Campbell, M., and Burton, V. 1994. Learning in their own style. *Science and Children* (April): 22–24, 29.

Available on NSTA Pathways to the Science Standards: Resources for the Road CD-ROM; *for information on the CD, go to* http://store.nsta.org.

Colburn, A., and Echevarria, J. 1999. Meaningful lessons. *The Science Teacher* 66 (3): 36–40. Reprinted in NSTA Press. 2001. *Celebrating Cultural Diversity: Science Learning for All.* Arlington, VA: NSTA Press.

Dunn, R. S., and Dunn, K. J. 1978. *Teaching Students Through Their Individual Learning Styles: A Practical Approach.* Reston, VA: Reston Publishing Co.

Gardner, H. 1983. *Frames of Mind: The Theory of Multiple Intelligences.* New York: Basic Books.

Gardner, H. 1999. *Intelligence Reframed: Multiple Intelligences for the 21st Century.* New York: Basic Books.

Hamm, D. 2002. Personal communication, 5 June.

National Association for Gifted Children (NAGC). 2002. Who Are the Gifted? In Parent Information [Web page], Washington, DC: National Association for Gifted Children. Retrieved February 21, 2002, from *http://www.nagc.org/ParentInfo/index.html.*

Simons, G. H., and Hepner, N. 1992. The special student in science. *Science Scope* (Sept.): 34–39, 54.

Spurlin, Q. 1995. Making science comprehensible for language minority students. *Journal of Science Teacher Education* 6(2): 71–78.

Thompson, B. R., and MacDougall, G. D. 2002. Intelligent teaching. *The Science Teacher* (Jan.): 44–48.

Learning Theories

As is the case with the other chapters in this book, each entry in this chapter should stand on its own. However, more than in other chapters, the ideas presented here tend to build on each other. Ideas that began with Piaget were later changed and expanded upon by others, as we shall see.

Piaget Jean Piaget was a Swiss psychologist who lived most of his life in the 20th century. He is generally considered the father of learning theory. Although learning psychologists have modified his ideas through the years, many of the basic tenets remain. Piaget began his work via observations of his own children, later expanding to observations of other children. He noted that infants, children, and adolescents understood and perceived the world quite differently from one another. Further, a natural progression existed from infant-like ways of understanding right up through more advanced adult ways of understanding, and we all progress—or develop—through the same stages of reasoning abilities.

Infants live in a world of sensory impressions. As young children, they begin developing abilities to understand, think, and generalize about objects, even when the objects are not present. Adults have these abilities, as well as more advanced reasoning skills. Adults can think about highly abstract ideas (including many science concepts). Piaget's great contribution was to conceive of thinking abilities as progressing developmentally.

We are constantly presented with new ideas—in and out of school. Learning is essentially a process of comparing the new ideas with the mental "maps" we've created of how everything works. If the new ideas fit well with our mental maps, then we easily "assimilate" the new learning. On the other hand, if the new learning doesn't fit well with our mental maps, then learning involves a process of "accommodating" the new ideas (or ignoring them—deciding that they just don't make sense or are in error). I'll further explain and expand upon some of Piaget's key ideas in other entries in this chapter.

Although Piaget's general ideas are still accepted throughout the education community, some of his ideas have been modified after further research. For example, almost no one continues to think that the reasoning stages Piaget proposed progress in as age-dependent a way as Piaget initially thought. We recognize extensive variation from person to person. In addition, many (though not all) in the education community have moved away from the idea that thinking structures are as generalized as Piaget thought. A person may be capable of rather abstract thinking in one situation yet be unable to think that way in a different situation. Generally speaking, the more unfamiliar a situation, the less likely a per-

son is to be able to think about it abstractly. This point is important to secondary science teachers because science classrooms represent very unfamiliar ideas and situations to most students.

cognitive development

The word "cognitive" (or "cognition") applies to the activities of the brain—thinking, in other words. Cognition is a general term that spans the gamut of brain activities from high-level, abstract reasoning all the way through imagination and how we use language, remember things, and perceive what's around us.

"Development," in turn, refers to change—usually change in some specified direction or path. Put together, "cognitive development" is the phrase we use when discussing how people's thinking abilities change over time. Piaget's explanation, that we progress from sensorimotor to preoperational to concrete and formal operational reasoning, is a theory of cognitive development. When we talk about cognitive development we're often (a) discussing whether a child's development is where we believe it "should" be at a particular life stage, (b) matching curricula to students' cognitive development (see "developmentally appropriate curricula," p. 57) or (c) challenging or trying to advance students' cognitive development to a "higher" level. This last point is probably synonymous with what people are talking about if you hear them discussing mental and intellectual growth.

Most people who study cognitive development believe it comes about through a combination of hereditary (or "built-in") factors, environmental factors, and interactions between the two. Most also believe that cognitive development is not something that can be represented as a single entity (like an IQ test score) and that our cognitive abilities vary according to context. This last point means, essentially, that a person's cognitive abilities can appear to be highly "advanced" in, say, a familiar environment where he or she has lots of experience, yet apparently less advanced in an unfamiliar environment or when he or she is confronted with certain new tasks.

concrete reasoning, formal reasoning The

concepts of concrete and formal reasoning also come from Piaget's work. It would be technically more accurate to discuss the "concrete operational stage of cognitive development" and the "formal operational state of cognitive development." We use "concrete operations" when describing what we observe or when we otherwise try to make sense of our experiences. These kinds of mental processes contrast with "formal operations," required in more complex scientific problem solving—as well as other

situations. Formal reasoning lets adolescents and adults go beyond descriptions to create and test hypothetical explanations for patterns they observe.

My discussion is rather simplified but, for purposes of this work, "concrete reasoning" refers to the kinds of mental processes we use when thinking about visible (or observable) entities. Formal reasoning concerns theoretical or nonobservable ideas or concepts. Electrical circuits, pendulums, and parts of a flower are concrete, observable entities. More abstract ideas, such as voltage, center of mass, beauty, or justice, are not. To truly understand these ideas one must possess formal reasoning abilities.

There's a certain arbitrariness in trying to divide the world into concrete and abstract entities. Concrete things often have abstract elements. For example, a habitat is the environment where a group of organisms normally lives. We can see many examples of habitats—in that sense, it's a rather concrete idea. Still, there's a certain amount of abstraction involved in going from the observation of sample habitats to understanding the more general concept.

A similar point can be made about geology's central idea, plate tectonics. On the one hand, fault lines are clearly visible, as is the evidence of land movement after an earthquake. Much of the thinking required to understand the concept of plate tectonics is quite concrete. Still, some amount of abstract reasoning is involved in trying to understand the idea that solid Earth is mobile and floating on melted rocks. Many ideas that seem highly contrary to our everyday life experience—including lots of scientific explanations—are abstract (our everyday experiences are lived within a mostly concrete world).

Perhaps you can see why I tend to think of concreteness and abstractness more as ranges than absolutes. Scientific ideas tend to be more (or less) concrete, more (or less) abstract.

The reason this distinction is important for teachers in middle and high schools is that students at those levels vary in their abilities to work with these two classes of ideas. Most middle and high school students are fairly adept at understanding concrete concepts. The same, however, cannot be said about more abstract ideas. In fact, education research suggests that many adults are rather challenged when thinking about some abstract ideas. If you think about it, we've had little need for abstract reasoning during much of human history— hunters and gatherers, for example, were often little concerned with philosophical and other (so-called) high-level thinking. Abstract reasoning is required to truly understand many scientific concepts. It's not required for large parts of everyday life—or at least hasn't been, historically, until recently.

Thus, teachers should be aware that their classes include students presently lacking the abilities to understand the highly abstract aspects of some scientific ideas. The more concrete an idea is, the more likely a majority of students in the class are able to understand it. This viewpoint provides a way to think about student abilities (which change with age and experience) and also a way in which to analyze the curriculum.

Consider pendulums, for example, a topic often taught in middle school physical science and high school physics courses. I started this entry by saying that pendulums represent a concrete idea. Indeed, pendulum, frequency (i.e., swings per minute), and period (i.e., seconds per swing) are all ideas that seem to be mostly concrete. How the pendulum's frequency varies with length and bob mass are also mostly concrete ideas. To a large extent, students can *see* all five of these concepts.

To appreciate fully the scientist's understanding of the relationship between frequency and pendulum length, however, requires understanding the theoretical concept of center of mass. A pendulum would behave similarly if its mass were concentrated at a single point, the center of mass, as it does in its visible or actual appearance. In working with formulas relating frequency and length, the physicist is working with a length from the pendulum's apex to its center of mass. That's a lot more abstract than the previous ideas.

Significantly, understanding *how* scientists understand relationships between pendulum frequency and length, mass, etc. requires understanding things like how and why scientists control variables when doing investigations, as well as understanding proportionality (two variables may be directly proportional, inversely proportional, exponentially proportional, etc.). If a student is currently unable to understand the idea of a variable, the need for controlling variables, or the concept of proportionality, then he or she will not truly understand what's happening with pendulum behavior.

So, it's fair to predict that most (older) students will understand the concrete ideas—including a qualitative understanding of the relationship between pendulum length and frequency—but some will struggle with formulas representing relationships between pendulum variables and ideas requiring understanding center of mass.

The same kind of analysis leads to the prediction that more students studying electricity will readily understand the concrete, or demonstrable, concepts of circuit, series circuit, and parallel circuit than the less concrete ideas of current and voltage, not to mention relationships between current, voltage, and resistance.

developmentally appropriate curricula are curricula that are matched to students' abilities. Techni-

cally, developmental appropriateness could refer to students' abilities in just about any area—emotional development, behavioral development, and so forth. Practically speaking, though, developmental appropriateness almost always refers to cognitive development (see "cognitive development," p. 54).

From a Piagetian perspective, a developmentally appropriate curriculum might focus on simple sensory experiences for the youngest of children, whereby they would experience and learn about concepts such as "wet" and "dry" or "tall" and "short." Children who are a little older would generally have the ability to start understanding and working with some of the ideas in their heads. For most elementary school students, and a fairly significant fraction of middle and high school students, a developmentally appropriate curriculum would focus heavily on learning new ideas via experiences—that is, it would be a hands-on curriculum whose ideas could generally be observed. Within the realm of scientific ideas, then, some older children and adults would find curricula that included working with abstract mental ideas to be developmentally appropriate. For some students, though, a curriculum requiring abstract mental reasoning about "invisible" ideas like atoms or genes would not be developmentally appropriate.

Sometimes people discuss the idea of developmental appropriateness without explicitly using that phrase. For

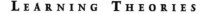

example, California's state science framework from the 1980s was something of a precursor to documents such as the *National Science Education Standards* (NRC 1996) and Project 2061's *Benchmarks for Science Literacy* (AAAS 1993) (both these documents are discussed in Chapter 10). The California framework included a section discussing developmentally appropriate curricula, but in terms of classic science process skills. "Observing" was discussed as a skill that could be practiced and developed in all students from kindergarten on up. Skills such as "categorizing" and "ordering" are better developed in slightly older children. Skills such as "controlling variables" and critiquing science investigations, to a large extent, are reserved for more developed students—teenagers or young adults, typically. Thus, a curriculum in which third graders were supposed to be setting up experiments and strictly controlling variables would probably not be considered to be developmentally appropriate by the authors of the California document.

This example is worth mentioning not only because the authors were discussing issues of developmental appropriateness, but also because they were doing so without focusing on specific science content. Their focus began with science process skills. Thus, discussion about what is more and less developmentally appropriate for children need

not be limited to science content.

At the risk of complicating the issue for readers, learning theorists today would probably say that the developmental appropriateness of curricula for a child will depend on *both* content and cognitive process skills. Students can sometimes make use of seemingly more advanced process skills if they are dealing with really familiar content.

constructivism has multiple meanings, and it's important that when people discuss the concept they be sure they're talking about the same thing! Much of the confusion stems from the fact that constructivism refers to both an explanation (theory) about how people learn and a philosophical position related to the nature of learning (see Matthews 1994, 137–39). Increasingly, people are also using the term to refer to teaching techniques designed to build on what students already know, for example, open-ended, hands-on inquiry (Brooks and Brooks 1993).

I'd like to focus on constructivism as an explanation about learning; that's probably what is most relevant to readers. In this context, "constructivism" refers to the concept that learners always bring with them to the classroom (or any other place where learning takes place) ideas about how the world works—including ideas related to whatever may be in today's lesson. Most of the time learners are unaware they even have these ideas! The ideas come from life experiences combined with what people have learned elsewhere.

According to constructivist learning theory, learners test new ideas against that which they already believe to be true. If the new ideas seem to fit in with their pictures of the world, they have little difficulty learning the ideas. There's no guarantee, though, that they will fit the ideas into their pictures of how the world works with the kind of meaning the teacher intends. (See the next two entries, "misconceptions" and "conceptual change.")

On the other hand, if the new ideas don't seem to fit the learner's picture of reality then they won't seem to make sense. Learners may dismiss them, learn them well enough to please the teacher (but never fully accept the ideas), or eventually accommodate the new ideas and change the way they understand the world. As you might guess, this third outcome is most difficult to achieve, although it's what teachers most often desire in students.

Seen this way, teaching is a process of trying to get people to change their minds—difficult enough as is, but made even more difficult by the fact that learners may not even know they hold an opinion about the idea in question! People who study learning and cognition often contrast constructivism with the more classical idea that students in our classes are "blank slates" who know nothing

about the topics they are being taught. From this perspective, the teacher "transmits" new information to students, who mentally store it away. In contrast, constructivist learning theory says that students are not blank slates; learning is sometimes a process whereby new ideas help students to "rewrite" the misconceptions already on their slates.

misconceptions In the

previous entry, about constructivism, I said that learners always bring preconceived ideas with them to the classroom about how the world works. Misconceptions, in the field of science education, are preconceived ideas that differ from those currently accepted by the scientific community. Educators use a variety of phrases synonymously with "misconceptions," including "naive conceptions," "prior conceptions," "alternate conceptions," and "preconceptions." Many people have interviewed students to discover commonly held scientific ideas (Driver, Guesne, and Tiberghien 1985; Osborne and Freyberg 1985).

One well-known example relates to how people explain what causes the seasons. People commonly say that the Earth revolves around the Sun, in an ellipse-shaped path, and that the Sun is at one of the ellipse's foci. Note that this idea is congruent with the scientifically accepted explanation and probably represents something students learned in school (or another educational setting). People then go on to say that during the part of Earth's orbit when the planet is closer to the Sun, we have summer and when the planet is farther from the Sun we have winter (Schneps 1987). This part of the explanation differs from that which is currently accepted as scientifically true. The "correct" explanation relates to the Earth's angle compared to the light coming from the Sun. Note also that, technically, the Earth's path around the Sun is elliptical, but astronomers will tell you the path is very close to being circular.

It's easy to see where this misconception could come from. It explains the seasons, and it jibes with what we've been taught in school. Problems only arise when one tries to explain things like how it is that half the Earth can experience summer while the other half is experiencing winter.

As another example of a misconception, consider the concept of biological adaptation. People tend to see adaptation as the way an individual organism changes to better fit its surroundings. Organisms change, people say, because the changes help them survive and reproduce. Polar bears adapted to their surroundings, becoming white, because the camouflage helped them be less visible to predators and also their prey. Both these factors helped them to survive.

As with the previous example on the seasons, readers will note echoes of ideas taught in school, as well as ideas fitting most people's picture of reality (what you might call "common sense"). There are, however, ideas within this explanation that are different from the scientifically accepted explanation.

Part of the difficulty stems from the way we use the word "adapt." The word is used differently in science and everyday life. In everyday life, individuals adapt to the changes that occur in their surroundings. We "get used to" things, learn to live with changes. This, however, is not biological adaptation. To the biologist, adaptations are the product of natural selection. The process begins with random mutations, followed by nature selecting some changes over others. It's a two-step process. In addition, adaptations are characteristics of a population. What's important, biologically, is that all polar bears are white. One bear that looks different from the rest is not spoken of as having a new adaption.

Notice again, though, that the common misconception about adaptation makes sense, in its own way, and is definitely not a reflection of lack of intelligence. It's actually a pretty good example of a common source of misconceptions—sometimes words are used differently in and out of science. "Adaptation" is an example of this. Biological adaptation is quite different from the kind of adaptation individual people do every day. Can you see how a student would hear about adaptation in science class, try to fit the idea in with what he or she already knows about (nonbiological) adaptation, and take away from class the misconception I just discussed?

conceptual change
If you've read the previous two entries, on constructivism and misconceptions, then this entry should follow naturally for you. Briefly I discussed the ideas that learning involves a process of comparing new ideas with our pictures of reality and sometimes changing this picture to accommodate the new ideas. Some of the ideas people commonly hold about how the world works may differ from those commonly accepted by the scientific community, even though the ideas work well for the individual who holds them.

With this backdrop, then, "conceptual change" simply refers to the process learners go through when they have experiences that challenge and change their thinking—going from a preconceived idea to a scientifically accepted (or "correct") idea.

Most people who study conceptual change see it as a process whereby people become more aware of their thinking about an idea, start to see problems with their thinking, and then choose an explanation that works better. This may seem straightforward, but research consistently shows conceptual change is difficult (Watson and Konicek 1990). Changing one idea may ultimately require a person to

change several ideas—something no one does easily.

Referring back to the last entry, about misconceptions, consider a student who believes that seasons are caused by variable distances between the Earth and Sun. Remember that this student could be a teenager or even an adult who has heard "correct" explanations in other science courses many times. People don't change their thinking simply because an authority figure presents a different explanation.

Consider a class, though, where the teacher has asked students about how they would explain what causes the seasons, and assume that some students mentioned the misconception I previously discussed. This might be a good time for the teacher to subtly challenge student thinking by asking a question or two related to the fact that the northern and southern hemispheres don't share seasons. Any good explanation for the seasons must be able to explain how winter in one hemisphere accompanies summer in the other hemisphere. If students were familiar with this fact, and if they seem puzzled, then the time is ripe for the teacher to introduce the new explanation and help students see why the scientifically accepted explanation is more fruitful than the other explanation. (As a side point related to the entries in this chapter about Piaget and concrete and formal reasoning, the teacher could probably help more students learn by having realistic models showing students how the Earth revolves around the Sun, demonstrating the scientifically accepted explanation for seasons.)

Before leaving this topic, I'd like readers to note that I have not prescribed any suggestions here about *how* to accomplish these changes. I only discussed the general ideas of teachers helping students to understand their personal preconceived ideas, create dissatisfaction with the ideas (if needed), develop different explanations, and see why the alternates are superior. These elements make up the conceptual change model. The model, however, relates to how people learn, with some clear-cut—but very general—implications for teachers. Neither constructivism nor conceptual change implies any single way to teach students. There are many ways teachers can help students change their thinking.

zone of proximal growth/zone of proximal development

These phrases are associated with the work of Russian psychologist Lev Vygotsky. Vygotsky was a contemporary of Piaget who died young (age 38), in 1934. In recent decades, however, his work has become better known and, to some, almost sounds contemporary. Like Piaget, Vygotsky sought to explain how we develop our thinking abilities.

Vygotsky's work distinguishes between the natural, unlearned mental abilities with which we are born and higher-thinking abilities that develop later. These higher-thinking abilities, in turn, are all dependent on language. Language makes thought possible. And language is a cultural phenomenon. Thus, his work included a lot of discussion about the role of language in regulating our behavior and our thinking. It's our ability, basically, to talk to ourselves—our inner speech—that makes higher thinking possible.

If you've followed this discussion so far, you're ready for the concept of "zone of proximal growth," the heading for this entry. Vygotsky said that every child has a sphere or a zone of current capabilities—a zone of proximal growth. Children of equal ages may have different abilities to answer questions.

Despite the fancy sounding phrase, this idea probably strikes readers as being so well-known as to be almost common sense. Remember, though, that when Vygotsky proposed the idea—in the first quarter of the 20th century—it was far from being common sense. In fact, even Piaget initially conceived of mental abilities as developing by age more than any other factors. Science teachers are probably aware of age-old debates about the importance of heredity versus environment in making us who we are. Vygotsky was among the key people to place a great importance on environment—particularly language, culture, and interactions between people. Thus, Vygotsky's work predicts that schools can do a lot to enhance children's thinking abilities by paying special attention to their language development. He also posits that schools, families, and other social settings can profoundly influence children's cognitive development—intelligence is not fixed at birth or even infancy, Vygotsky adherents would say.

scaffolding
I discussed the idea that Vygotsky called the zone of proximal development in the last entry. The phrase refers to the range of knowledge and skills students are not yet ready to learn on their own, but could learn with help from teachers.

"Scaffolding" refers to continually challenging students within their zones of proximal development, while making it possible for them to meet the challenges by providing the kind of teaching, guidance, and feedback to ensure they're successful with reasonable effort.

Scaffolding is a general term applying to the whole range of assistance or simplification strategies teachers use to bridge the gap between what students can do on their own and what they can do with help. Just like the scaffolds that builders use, these instructional scaffolds are meant to be temporary structures taken away when they are no longer needed. The idea is to help students complete assignments and other school tasks but not provide so much help that the teacher ends up doing the tasks for the students. The teacher provides just the minimum that students need to do the tasks for themselves.

Consider a lecture, for example. Some students may have difficulty following what the teacher discusses in the lecture or learning via note taking. These students might be successful, however, if the teacher merely provided a brief outline of the lecture and cued students in on the kinds of things that they should write in their notes. This is different, though, from the teacher telling students everything they should write or providing a set of lecture notes. The teacher is helping students but not doing all the work or providing all the "answers" for his or her students.

Note that in the previous paragraph I referred to "some" students, not all students. The scaffold concept is something that refers to individual students. Technically, each student might require a different kind of scaffold (even though that is not what happens in practice, especially with larger classes). In addition, remember that the scaffold is meant to be temporary. In the lecture example, the teacher would not be providing lecture notes or hints all year—just until students were able to be successful without the external help. At that point the teacher would remove the scaffold and probably move on to challenging students in some new way.

REFERENCES & FURTHER INFORMATION:

American Association for the Advancement of Science (AAAS). 1993. *Benchmarks for Science Literacy*. New York: Oxford University Press.

Bransford, R., Brown, A. L., and Cocking, R. R., eds. 1999. *How People Learn: Brain, Mind, Experience, and School*. Washington, DC: National Academy Press. [available online at *http://stills.nap.edu/readingroom/books/howpeople1/*]

Brooks, J. G., and Brooks, M. G. 1993. *In Search of Understanding: The Case for Constructivist Classrooms*. Alexandria, VA: Association for Supervision and Curriculum Development.

Driver, R., Guesne, E., and Tiberghien, A. 1985. *Children's Ideas in Science*. Buckingham, England: Open University Press.

Matthews, M. R. 1994. *Science Teaching: The Role of History and Philosophy of Science*. New York: Routledge.

National Research Council (NRC). 1996. *National Science Education Standards*. Washington, DC: National Academy Press.

Osborne, R., and Freyberg, P. 1985. *Learning in Science*. Portsmouth, NH: Heinemann.

Schneps, M. H. 1987. *A Private Universe*. (videotape) Available from Pyramid Films and Video, 2801 Colorado Avenue, Santa Monica, CA 90404.

Watson, B., and Konicek, R. 1990. Teaching for conceptual change: Confronting children's experience. *Phi Delta Kappan* (May): 680–85.

Research Concepts

qualitative research

generally involves a researcher combining observation, interviews, and analysis of various documents. These methods are derived from the kinds of research methods generally used by anthropologists. Colloquially, some people think of such methods as merely "research without numbers." Properly done, though, qualitative research studies can be quite rigorous and enlightening.

One example of a study falling under the "qualitative" categorization would be an ethnography of a classroom. Ethnographies are long-term studies strongly associated with anthropology. The purpose of this type of study might be to provide readers with a student's view of life within the "culture" of an urban school where most students drop out. As outsiders looking in, we might wonder, Why would capable, smart students purposely choose to do poorly in school?

The qualitative researcher approaching this question would spend many weeks or months observing classes, hallways, lunchrooms, and other settings within and around the school. The researcher would make every attempt to be objective and unbiased in his or her observations—including probably trying to become more aware of biases he or she brings to the situation. The researcher would be looking for patterns within the observations that lend understanding of the research question. To give the work validity, the researcher would not only try to support conclusions with multiple observations; he or she would also try to use multiple sources for information, interviewing many students, as well as teachers, coaches, and parents, for example. If the same conclusions seem to come from multiple data sources, then the conclusions are more likely to be valid than if they only came from a single data source.

Qualitative studies are frequently not as generalizable as other types of studies, but that's not their purpose. Instead, researchers aim to provide a kind of insight or deep understanding that is impossible through other research means.

quantitative

research represents the kind of

research many teachers associate with education research. Quantitative studies often try to follow the kinds of experimental methods natural scientists and psychologists use in their work. Quantitative studies almost always rely on statistical procedures as part of their data analysis.

Consider, for instance, the issue I used as an example in the previous entry. A researcher might wonder whether it was possible to identify early on those students who are at-risk of dropping out, with the ultimate goal of working with those students to decrease their chance of dropping out. To accomplish this, the researcher might begin by trying to create a matched pair of student groups—one group who dropped out of school and another group who didn't. The value of the study would probably hinge on how well "matched" the two groups were. In a well-done study, the two groups would be as alike as possible, except for the fact that one group dropped

out and the other did not. In addition, the researchers would make clear the thinking and procedures they used in determining what constituted matched groups.

Once this was done, the researchers could then go back to, for example, the various standardized tests students took or the grades they received in sixth grade. The researchers would be looking for statistically significant differences between these two groups in their grades and/or their test scores. The researchers might conclude that the differences they found were linked, or correlated, to the probability that one group of students would later drop out; the researchers could use that information to identify current students in need of extra attention.

In this entry and the previous entry, on qualitative research, I tried to set my examples up to be congruent. Both examples relate to questions about students dropping out of school. Both questions represent important topics that are worthy of research. However, the questions are very different from one another. Different kinds of questions call for different kinds of research methods when trying to answer them. Both qualitative and quantitative research have important roles to play in deepening our understanding of the education issues we all find important. In fact, the qualitative study might help quantitative researchers decide the kinds of factors they should be looking at as potentially being linked to later dropping out. Similarly, the quantitative research might help the qualitative researchers identify whom or where they should be observing. The studies would complement one another.

action research is more

personal or local than the traditional quantitative or qualitative research I described above. With the previous kinds of research, the researchers are interested in their work being applicable in some form or another beyond the confines of a single school or classroom. Teachers doing action research projects, on the other hand, are generally more focused on work whose ultimate value is local (e.g., their classroom, school, or district). They'll use the results themselves. Although the work may form the basis for a graduate thesis, authors are generally less concerned with the work being applicable enough for publication in research journals than are those engaged in other kinds of education research.

Action research projects usually begin when an individual teacher (or other school professional) identifies a question or problem that's personally relevant and then collects and analyzes information to answer the question. A simple action research project one chemistry teacher conducted began with his concern about how difficult it was to get his students to wear their goggles during laboratory activities. His research question was "Why don't my students wear their goggles?" The questionnaires and interviews he did with

students led him to the conclusion, in this case, that students perceived they didn't need to wear goggles because the school wouldn't really allow dangerous chemicals to be present in classrooms.

In another case, a teacher wondered whether teaching students how to make concept maps and then requiring students to make concept maps (in place of other assignments) would result in students performing better on chapter quizzes. By keeping records that let her compare student work before and after the change, she too was doing an action research project.

As a final example, consider a teacher who noticed that the boys and girls in a class performed differently. The teacher was concerned that this difference might be due to students receiving different amounts of attention—those with higher performance getting more teacher attention. To test whether there was support for the idea, the teacher invited colleagues with a free period to visit the classroom and observe how much time the teacher spent with boys versus girls, as well as the nature of the interactions. Tallying data from class after class, the teacher was able to get a lot of information about how much time was spent with the two groups.

As the last example shows, action research doesn't have to be done alone; others can be involved. In fact, multiple teachers could be looking at the same question, working collaboratively.

validity
In classical educational research studies (as well as tests and other assessment instruments), "validity" refers to the extent to which the study (or test) measures what the researchers say it measures. A valid test of ninth graders' science knowledge would be one that actually measures ninth graders' science knowledge. It's so intuitive as to be obvious that good studies need to be valid. Keep in mind, though, that the test might measure what ninth graders are supposed to know about science, but if the ninth graders in your district weren't taught the stuff that's being assessed, then this test is *not* valid for your students.

When people discuss validity, they are usually talking about a test, questionnaire, or survey of some sort. However, for a study to be valid, the study must be valid throughout. Let's look at that ninth-grade test as an example. Suppose for the moment that the test actually is a valid measure of what ninth graders should know and be able to do in your state. The state might decide to find out how its ninth graders are doing. The state, however, may not have the money to test every student. Instead, state officials might opt to test a representative sample of students. The overall validity of the study, then, will depend not only on how valid the test is, but also on the validity of the students sampled. If the students who take the test are not highly representative of the state as a whole, then the results of the study might be deemed by other researchers to be lacking in validity (or to be invalid). Thus, this study's validity for its intended purpose depends on *both* the test's validity *and* the sample's validity.

reliability
Along with validity, reliability represents the other aspect of a research study that people most often discuss when evaluating the study. Reliability is an estimate of how closely the results of a test (or questionnaire, survey, etc.) would match if the test were given repeatedly to the same student under the same conditions. If I took a test three days in a row and got wildly different scores each time, we would say the test was not a reliable measure. Clearly, if a test is designed to measure something that shouldn't be varying day to day, then a good test would not produce a result that varied day to day.

"Inter-rater reliability" is a related concept that researchers discuss frequently when people work on studies involving observation of a classroom (or other educational setting). Large or well-funded studies may involve multiple people observing one or more classrooms, coding the teachers' behaviors. For example, a study might involve a checklist where the observer checks off each time he or she sees the teacher exhibit a particular behavior. If this is a good study, you would expect that two people observing the same classroom teacher at the same time would produce checklists with similar results. In this case, researchers would say the inter-rater reliability was high.

Besides studies with two or more people observing the same setting, it's also common for studies to include multiple people observing multiple classrooms—you and I would be looking at different classrooms at different times, using the same checklist. Again, a quality study would need high inter-rater reliability. People looking at the study's results need to know that what you and I considered "teacher asks a short-answer question" was the same thing. What usually happens in these instances is that the various observers will be trained in how to observe, using whatever checklist they are supposed to use, and assessed to be sure they code similarly to their trainer(s). That's how the researchers will establish high inter-rater reliability.

Likert scale
Likert scales are extremely common in surveys. People filling out the survey are asked a question or asked the extent to which they agree with a statement. They respond on a scale—for example, 1 = strongly agree, 2 = moderately agree, . . . 5 = strongly disagree. Educational researchers call this a Likert scale, in honor of Rensis Likert, who is credited with the idea.

A Likert scale can have any number of response choices. Having an odd number of choices—for example, 1, 2, 3, 4, 5—leaves respondents the option of choosing a response that's often set up to be neutral. In this example, that would probably be response 3. If there's an even number of choices—for example, 1, 2, 3, 4—the people creating the survey force respondents to make firmer decisions about their viewpoints.

sample, sampling
Sampling is a term used in statistics. Quantitative studies rely on statistics, and evaluating those studies often requires statistical understanding. One of the key ideas in statistics is that of a "sample." When one wants to find out information about a huge group—usually called a "population"—it's impractical to work with everyone in the group. Instead, the researcher will work with a subset of the group—a sample—and results will then be generalized to everyone in the group.

An example will make the idea easier to understand. Suppose you wanted to find out whether listening to music while studying affects students' grades. You decide to work with two groups—students who listen to music for more than five hours per week while studying and students who don't listen to music at all while studying. You ask members of each group about their grades (and assume you get accurate information). Next, you set up your study conditions so that the groups will be similar in other ways (this is necessary for your study to be "fair," that is, scientifically controlled). Within those two groups, however, are probably millions of students throughout the world. Even if you limited your study to students in the United States, you'd still have way too many students to survey.

Thus, you'll need to get information from a sample—one group that will represent all the students who listen to a lot of music and another group that will represent all the students who listen to no music. The value of your study will hinge on two factors. First, you have to be sure the samples you use are representative of the larger populations being exemplified. The group of students you sample who don't listen to music, for example, must be statistically the same as the overall group of nonlisteners. A famous example of a sample that was *not* statistically the same comes from the 1948 U.S. presidential election, where polls predicted a victory for Thomas Dewey. As it turned out, the people sampled for the poll—each of whom had been telephoned—were not statistically the same as the population of voters—some of whom did not have telephones. The result was different than that predicted; Truman won.

Second, besides ensuring that the sample is representative of the overall population, you also have to be sure to sample a large enough group to get representative data. In other words, how many people you sample is important. It's beyond the scope of this book to discuss how many people you need to sample— the answer depends on how accurate and confident you need to be. However, it is a topic discussed in most college statistics courses.

One last point. Even if you've got a great sample, one that's really big, you probably won't find a number that's exactly the same as you would get if you got information from everyone in the population. You will, however, be really close! Statisticians and educational researchers always talk about ranges. They wouldn't say, for example, that the students who listened to a lot of music averaged 78 percent in their science classes; instead, they might say something like, "We concluded, with 95 percent confidence, that students who listened to a lot of music averaged between 76 percent and 80 percent in their science classes." (Translated, that means "If we repeated the procedure with 100 samples from this population, we would expect that average to be somewhere between 76 percent and 80 percent for 95 of the samples.") The more people in the sample, the closer the results will be to those of the "actual" population, and the smaller will be the range of scores discussed by the researchers. For example, if the sample were bigger, the researchers might conclude that the example score above was between 77 percent and 79 percent. Statistics is devoted to questions and issues such as those I have discussed in this entry.

(statistically) significant difference I discussed the idea
of a statistical sample in the previous

entry and used as an example a study comparing students who listened to music for more than five hours a week while studying to students who didn't listen to any music while studying. This study was a way of addressing the question of whether listening to music while studying was linked to grades. Reading that entry might help you understand this one.

There's always a certain amount of chance statistical fluctuation whenever a researcher samples a population and uses the information to generalize about a larger group. That's why researchers express their results as a *range* rather than an absolute number, like 76–80 percent rather than 78 percent. If two scores are different in a way that is statistically significant, that just means their ranges don't overlap. Suppose, for instance, that the second group in the example study I've been using has a scholastic average of 83 percent. If the sample were the same size as the first group, the researchers would express the score as being somewhere in the range of 81–85 percent (83±2 percent). The ranges don't overlap, and it's clear that these figures differ from one another.

Consider, however, the case where the students who studied quietly had an average scholastic grade of 81 percent. The reported range would be 79–83 percent (81±2 percent)—the actual population of all students almost certainly has an average score somewhere within the range of 79–83 percent. The actual average could be anywhere within that range.

Because the actual score could be as low as 79 or 80 percent for this group, and the other group's score could be as high as 79 or 80 percent, we cannot conclude definitively—statistically—that the scores are actually different. So, even though one group averaged 78 and the other 81, we cannot conclude with any certainty that the actual populations—all the students in the country who study with lots of music or without music—truly differ in their science scores. The results are too close to call. Researchers would say the difference between the scores is *not* statistically significant.

REFERENCES & FURTHER INFORMATION:

Loucks-Horsley, S., Love, N., Stiles, K. E., Mundry, S., and Hewson, P. W. 2003. *Designing Professional Development for Teachers of Science and Mathematics*. (2nd ed.) Thousand Oaks, CA: Corwin Press. (*See pp. 94–103 for information about action research.*)

Slavin, R. 2003. A reader's guide to scientifically based research. *Educational Leadership* 60 (5): 12–16.

Teacher Education

preservice teacher

is a generic term educators use when referring to student teachers and other prospective teachers during the period they are learning to teach as undergraduate or graduate students. Preservice teachers can be observing in the classroom, tutoring, helping the teacher, or teaching lessons under the classroom teacher's supervision.

These days, prospective teachers commonly have experiences in schools long before their formal student teaching. Borrowing from anthropology, teacher educators commonly call all school experiences "field experiences." It's a bit confusing sometimes to talk about students in a field experience—is the speaker discussing K–12 students or university students? the listener wonders.

As it became increasingly common for teacher education students to spend time in K–12 schools before the time they spent student teaching, educators invented the term "preservice teacher" to clearly distinguish K–12 students from university students. The term may also exist to help raise the status of prospective teachers to be nearer that of the classroom teacher.

inservice teacher University faculty often contrast preservice teachers with "inservice" teachers. The latter are regular classroom teachers—teachers legally responsible for the education of a group of K–12-level students. Inservice teachers are currently serving in their profession, whereas preservice teachers are enrolled in a formal program to become teachers.

supervising, cooperating, or mentor teacher The supervising, cooperating, or mentor teacher is the schoolteacher (inservice teacher) who formally acts as an adviser to a student teacher. The terms are interchangeable. If you have a student teacher in your classroom, then you are the supervising/cooperating/mentor teacher for that person.

Cooperating teachers often agree to work with a student teacher because they see it as a way to give back to the profession and influence the next generation of teachers. Some people view the experience as professional development—teaching another about how you teach almost forces you to become more reflective and aware of what you are doing and its impact on your students. In addition, many teachers like to have a student teacher in their classroom because they enjoy having another adult around; they may spend virtually all day with kids and enjoy the chance to talk about the joys and frustrations of their job with someone else.

professional development schools are also known as "clinical schools" or "professional practice schools." The terms are synonymous. A professional development school, or PDS, is meant to be the educational equivalent of a teaching hospital. Teaching hospitals bring together researchers, doctors, and doctors-in-training to offer cutting-edge medical developments to patients. Simultaneously they act as places where the next generation of health-care professionals is trained. As envisioned in the 1980s and 1990s, PDSs were to be similar—schools where K–12 teachers, university professors, and preservice teachers worked together. They would be doing educational research, teaching K–12 students, and training both new and experienced teachers. Researchers would have a laboratory for their work and K–12 teachers would have access to the latest research and all the resources a university has at its disposal. Meanwhile, university faculty and K–12 teachers would be training prospective teachers in real-life settings.

Another way to understand the PDS concept is to remember the idea of a lab school. Once found throughout the United States, today it's rare to find a state with more than one or two lab schools.

Lab schools are K–12 schools, on or near college campuses, that provide "labs" for the latest research and teaching techniques and for student teachers to learn their craft. The reason for their gradual disappearance, critics of the schools contend, is that most of the students were children of professors and other highly educated people working on a campus. Thus, research results were not applicable to other kinds of students, and student teachers were not well prepared to teach a more varied or typical student population. One can think of a PDS as being like a lab school that is populated by "typical" students, located in a more "typical" community setting—not on a college campus—and funded like other public schools.

PDSs seemed to represent a win-win situation for everyone involved. In practice, though, rhetoric has not always matched reality. Universities and K–12 schools are very different institutions with different goals and ways of rewarding faculty members for their work. It is difficult to blend their two cultures. It also seems to be rare to find a single site effectively combining K–12 teaching, prospective teacher training, inservice teacher professional development, and research. (The American Association of Colleges for Teacher Education and the Educational Resources Information Clearinghouse have useful background information about PDSs on the Web, available at *http://www.aacte.org/Eric/ eric_digest.htm.*)

Thus, readers must understand that operational definitions of PDSs don't always match the previous explanation. In other words, you may visit or hear about settings referred to as professional development schools that don't match what you just read. Usually, these PDSs have some of these elements but not all of them. For example, what's called a PDS might feature multiple university students taking classes and having other school experiences at a single school. The school, however, may have little research going on, especially research actively involving K–12 teachers as participants or even co-researchers. Another setting might feature close collaboration between university and K–12 faculty, but comparatively little preservice teacher education. Settings that borrow some features from the real model of a PDS aren't truly professional development schools. Nevertheless, participants might refer to these settings as professional development schools, which can cause confusion.

induction is the term university educators and K–12 administrators often use to refer to the time when a beginning teacher is making the transition from being a student teacher to being an experienced member of a school's staff. Besides learning basic teaching and classroom management skills, beginning teachers are also learning the ways of a new culture. As every experienced teacher knows, the first year or two in the classroom is when teachers learn a lot not only about teaching, but also how to be a teacher and a member of a school's staff.

People throughout the educational spectrum have long recognized the importance of the induction period and implemented various programs to support new teachers. Universities recognize there's only so much their faculty can effectively teach preservice teachers, especially before they've had relevant teaching experiences to draw on. K–12 schools recognize the value of helping new teachers understand the school in which they're teaching.

State and national politicians, too, believe that programs aimed at supporting new teachers—induction programs—will help new teachers be more successful and more likely to stay in the classroom than would be the case without assistance. Some states, for example, pay school districts to offer beginning teacher assistance. States may also have two-tiered credentials, with the more "advanced" credential being something that comes after one has taught for two to five years. Working for the secondary credential provides a kind of induction program because teachers at that level may need to take courses or workshops to further their education and teaching skills.

clinical supervision

is a process that was invented to be less evaluative than the process traditionally associated with teacher supervision. With clinical supervision, teachers receive information related to their teaching, which, in turn, they can use in making decisions about how to most effectively teach their students. If you've looked at Chapter 5, "Assessment," you'll understand what I mean when I say that traditional supervision is summative, whereas clinical supervision is meant to be formative.

The clinical supervision cycle has three phases. The process begins with a conference between the teacher and supervisor (or "observer"). The teacher orients the observer to what's going on in the classroom in general as well as to that day's lesson. A key part of this conference is a discussion about what the teacher would like the observer to focus on. For example, the teacher might be interested in learning the following about him- or herself: Am I asking the kinds of questions that get kids thinking? Do I then give students enough time to think before I start talking again? Does it sound as if I'm really listening and responding to what students say? Do I pick boys more often than girls to answer questions?

As science teachers, we might say that the lesson observation is analogous to data collection in a small research study. This is rather different from traditional supervision, since the observer is not really present for the purpose of judging the teacher's abilities. This lack of judgment-passing is a key reason that peer supervision—teachers observing each other—often follows a clinical supervision cycle.

After the lesson, the teacher and observer meet again. During this third phase of the clinical supervision cycle, the observer shares the data he or she collected. Through dialogue with the observer and reflection on the information provided by the observer, the teacher figures out how to modify his or her teaching. Thus, clinical supervision is meant to be a process that encourages teacher change, but does so in a way that's more reflective and internally motivated than traditional supervision.

professional development refers to the

opportunities offered to educators to "develop new knowledge, skills, approaches, and dispositions to improve their effectiveness in their classrooms and organizations" (Loucks-Horsley et al. 1998, p. xiv). Indeed, any activity that helps teachers develop within their profession is professional development. For example, teachers working together to examine student results and determine better ways to support student achievement is professional development. So are strategies such as teacher study groups, lesson study, case discussion, and self-reflection and inquiry.

"Professional development" also refers to the many specially designed workshops and institutes for educators. Furthermore, if you're reading this, there's

a good chance you're a member of the National Science Teachers Association (NSTA) (which published the book), so you probably know that another common professional development avenue comes from membership in professional organizations, reading their journals and books, and attending their conferences.

Teachers can also take college courses or earn graduate degrees as professional development. Online professional development courses are increasingly popular. For example, the NSTA Institute offers online courses tailored to science teachers. The institute *(www.nsta. org/institute)* partners with the National Teachers Enhancement Network (NTEN), the Jason Academy, and the University of Maryland's College of Life Sciences to offer a variety of K–12 science content courses.

modeling is a fancy word for a

simple idea—demonstrating. To model something is to show another person a behavior, skill, or attitude. A key point about this otherwise simple idea, though, is that the teacher modeling may be conscious or unconscious.

A teacher is consciously modeling when leading a district or in-school workshop where participants act as students to experience, say, what cooperative learning is about. When this same teacher goes back to her classroom and speaks gently to her class, trying never to embarrass students by publicly scolding them, she is still modeling, though it might be unconscious behavior on her part. She's modeling how people should treat each other. In fact, a classic study completed more than 50 years ago showed that students copy their teachers' behavioral patterns. If the teacher frequently yells at students, for example, students will eventually treat each other the same way (Anderson and Brewer 1946). The key point, though, is that students copy their teachers' behavior patterns, so teachers are always modeling—whether they are aware of it or not.

I decided to discuss the term "modeling" in the chapter on professional development because I probably hear the idea mentioned most often within the context of workshops conducted by a school or school district. Indeed, modeling teaching ideas is an integral part of many local workshops—before learning about a new teaching approach, it's helpful to have experienced what the approach is all about. Similarly, the practice of demonstration lessons as a professional development strategy—whereby an experienced teacher models a lesson for others—is also an example of modeling.

I could, though, just as easily have discussed modeling in Chapter 4, "Teaching Techniques." Modeling ultimately represents one of the most powerful teaching strategies available. Its implication for the teacher is simple: To be as effective as possible, you must be the kind of person you'd like your students to be,

and your students must regularly observe you being this way.

National Board Certification

The National Board for Professional Teaching Standards was born in the mid-1980s in the wake of a report by the President's Commission on Excellence in Education (1983) called *A Nation at Risk: The Imperative for Educational Reform*. The commission called for the teaching profession to set high teaching standards and certify teachers who met those standards. The result was the National Board for Professional Teaching Standards (NBPTS) and the beginning of National Board Certification, available to advanced teachers. Information about NBPTS and National Board Certification can be found online at *http://www.nbpts.org/about/hist.cfm*.

Most teachers find National Board Certification to be a lengthy, rigorous, but ultimately rewarding experience. The assessment is made up of two parts—a portfolio that candidates assemble outside of National Board facilities and exercises completed at a National Board assessment center. The portfolio is a measure of teaching in real-life settings. As such, it includes things such as videotapes a teacher makes of his or her teaching, samples of student work, lesson plans and other teaching artifacts, and—perhaps most importantly—essays that teacher candidates write to analyze their work.

These commentaries discuss the goals and purposes of instruction, reflections on what occurred, the effectiveness of the practice, and the rationale for the teacher's professional judgment. Most teachers take 200 to 400 hours to prepare their portfolios, and the National Board requires teachers to spend at least five months on the process. At the assessment center, teachers take tests designed to assess their content knowledge and other aspects of teaching. Some of the assessment items are nontraditional, that is, the testing involves more than answering multiple-choice questions or writing short responses to question prompts.

Teachers choose to attempt National Board Certification for a variety of reasons. The certification represents a mark of professional competence, recognition, and prestige. In some locations, National Board Certification also brings additional money to the recipient. A lot of teachers, though, find the experience of completing the application portfolios to be rewarding in and of itself—separate from what happens after receiving certification.

REFERENCES & FURTHER INFORMATION:

Anderson, H. H., and Brewer, H. M. 1946. Studies of teacher's classroom personality I: Dominative and socially integrative behavior of kindergarten teachers. *Applied Psychology Monographs* (6).

For more information on professional development for science teachers, take a look at the following:

American Association for the Advancement of Science (AAAS). 1997. *Resources for Science Literacy: Professional Development.* New York: Oxford University Press.

Loucks-Horsley, S., Love, N., Stiles, K. E., Mundry, S., and Hewson, P. W. 2003. *Designing Professional Development for Teachers of Science and Mathematics.* (2nd ed.) Thousand Oaks, CA: Corwin Press.

Rhoton, J., and Bowers, P., eds. 2001. *Professional Development: Planning and Design.* Arlington, VA: NSTA Press.

Rhoton, J., and Bowers, P., eds. 2001. *Professional Development Leadership and the Diverse Learner.* Arlington, VA: NSTA Press.

Rhoton, J., and Bowers, P., eds. 2003. *Science Teacher Retention: Mentoring and Renewal.* Arlington, VA: NSTA Press.

Documents

National Science Education Standards

The National Science Education Standards were published in 1996, after a lengthy commentary period from many interested citizens and groups. In the overview of the book, the authors write:

> *The intent of the* Standards *can be expressed in a single phrase: Science standards for all students.* (NRC 1996, 2)

The Standards were designed to be achievable by all students, no matter their background or characteristics. The next paragraph of the document's overview goes on to say:

> *Students cannot achieve high levels of performance without access to skilled professional teachers, adequate classroom time, a rich array of learning materials, accommodating work spaces, and the resources of the communities surrounding their schools. Responsibility for providing this support falls on all those involved with the science education system.* (2)

Emphases such as those just mentioned are reflected in the areas the Standards cover. Beside standards for science content and for science teaching, the *National Science Education Standards* includes standards for professional development for science teachers, science education programs, and even science education systems. Finally, the document also addresses what some consider the bottom line for educational reform—standards for assessment in science education.

Although the information in the *National Science Education Standards* is often written in a rather general manner, the resulting document provides a far-reaching and generally agreed upon comprehensive starting place for people interested in changing the U.S. science educational system.

Project 2061: Science for All Americans Project 2061: Benchmarks for Science Literacy

According to its website, "Project 2061 is the long-term initiative of the American Association for the Advancement of Science [AAAS] working to reform K–12 science, mathematics, and technology education nationwide" (*http://www. project2061.org*). AAAS is North America's largest scientific organization. It named its educational reform initiative Project 2061 in honor of the year Halley's comet will return to Earth. The association wanted to emphasize the idea that education reform is a lengthy, slow process that cannot happen overnight—and that AAAS's involvement would be long and sustained.

Project 2061 has devoted resources to a number of activities since its inception in 1985—workshops, conferences, newsletters, and various tools for educators. In this entry, however, I will dis-

cuss the two best-known documents to have emerged from the project.

Science for All Americans (SFAA) (1989) came first. The book, now available online (*http://www.project2061.org/tools/sfaaol/Intro.htm*), begins:

> *This book is about science literacy.* Science for All Americans *consists of a set of recommendations on what understandings and ways of thinking are essential for all citizens in a world shaped by science and technology.*

The ideas within the book, in some ways, were the beginning of the discussion that continues today among scientists and teachers at all levels about what K–12 students should understand regarding science.

SFAA was important on its own, but it was also important as a forerunner to the National Science Education Standards and AAAS's own *Benchmarks for Science Literacy* (1993). AAAS published *Benchmarks* four years after *SFAA*, but mentions both documents in the *Benchmarks* introduction (*Benchmarks* is available online at *http://www.project2061.org/tools/benchol/bchin.htm*):

> SFAA *answers the question of what constitutes adult science literacy, recommending what all students should know and be able to do in science, mathematics, and technology by the time they graduate from high school.* Benchmarks *specifies how students should progress toward science literacy, recom-*

mending what they should know and be able to do by the time they reach certain grade levels. Together, the two publications can help guide reform in science, mathematics, and technology education.

It's difficult to summarize *Benchmarks* in a handful of words; it's a rather large document. Basically, though, much of the document is made up of recommendations about what students should know and be able to do by the end of grades two, five, eight, and twelve. The work was put together with input from many people, but mostly K–12 teachers, administrators, and scientists. It's not meant to be used as a curriculum or even as a set of standards (depending on how the term is being used). Instead, it's meant to guide and help those engaged in creating curricula and standards. *Benchmarks* has been particularly influential, among other uses, as part of the basis for many states' science standards.

Project 2061 is still very active. More recent publications include *Blueprints for Reform* and *Atlas of Science Literacy* (see References & Further Information at the end of this chapter).

Scope, Sequence, and Coordination project

No large project is really the product of one person. However, many people associate the National Sci-

ence Teachers Association's (NSTA) Scope, Sequence, and Coordination (SS&C) project with Bill Aldridge. Aldridge was NSTA's executive director when the ideas behind SS&C were revealed to the public in the January 1989 issue of *NSTA Reports!* In the article, Aldridge discussed the need to broaden the U.S. pool of potential scientists and engineers via school experiences in middle and high school science and to increase students' general science literacy. In other words, he discussed the value of science for everyone, rather than just a select few who would go on to further science study.

Aldridge believed that traditional courses suffered from a lack of coordination, being highly abstract and theoretical, spending too little time on each subject, cramming lots of ideas into a limited amount of time, and, as a result, incorrectly teaching science. What was new, however, was what came next: To address these points, Aldridge proposed a radical revamping of the way science courses were structured, sequenced, and taught at the middle and high school levels.

Aldridge recommended that all students take science every year (his proposal came at a time when school districts all over the country were increasing their science requirements). Rather than a lot of science crammed into a couple of years during high school, every student would learn a little bit about each science subject (biology, chemistry, physics, Earth science) during every year from middle school through high school—that is, students would learn biology every year, chemistry every year, and so forth. The subjects would be taught in a coordinated way, with content moving from concrete ideas (taught in the middle school) to abstract ideas (taught later in high school) and would emphasize practical applications, asking questions, and critical thinking.

Experimental programs were created to test the implementation of the SS&C ideas in a few states and territories. Each state/territory experimented with a different way to achieve the SS&C vision. After a couple of years, results were mixed and funding for the project was eliminated. Consequently, the project no longer exists. Supporters claimed that funders provided insufficient time to see significant results—changes of this magnitude would take years—and that great pressure to achieve observable results hampered progress.

However, I think it's fair to say that the ideas behind the SS&C project are still alive and well in the form of widespread support for integrated and coordinated science. In fact, many districts in my own state of California refer to their integrated/coordinated science programs as "SS&C science."

"alphabet soup" curricula
When the Soviets launched the *Sputnik* satellite in the late 1950s, Americans were afraid that Russian dominance in areas such as aerospace would lead to diminished U.S. security. To counteract this, politicians and citizens believed the United States needed more scientists and engineers. The result was lots of money allotted to the U.S. Department of Defense for purposes of elementary and secondary science—the "Golden Age" for science education.

The products of this funding included many new curricula during the 1960s. Well-known elementary programs included the Elementary Science Study (ESS), the Science Curriculum Improvement Study (SCIS), and Science—A Process Approach (SAPA). The list of secondary science curricula is even longer, but included the Biological Sciences Curriculum Study (BSCS), ChemStudy, Physical Science Study Committee (PSSC), and Harvard Project Physics.

With so many curricula, usually referred to by their acronyms, people called the programs collectively a veritable "alphabet soup"—and the moniker has stuck to this day.

In fact, a remarkable number of the curriculum projects have also lasted to this day—more than 40 years later. Some of the projects, like BSCS, are alive and well. BSCS, in fact, continues to create new curricula. Some of the other curriculum projects are no longer in print, but their influence also continues. Many common laboratory activities, for example, have their roots in the various "alphabet soup" curricula. Some would even say that much of today's emphasis on the hands-on aspect of science instruction is due, at least in part, to these curriculum projects (although, in reality, educators have advocated hands-on lab instruction for many, many years).

REFERENCES & FURTHER INFORMATION:

American Association for the Advancement of Science (AAAS). 1989. *Science for All Americans*. New York: Oxford University Press. [available online at *http://2061.aaas.org/tools/sfaa/index.html*]

American Association for the Advancement of Science (AAAS). 1993. *Benchmarks for Science Literacy*. New York: Oxford University Press. [available online at *http://www.project 2061.org/tools/benchol/bolframe.htm*]

American Association for the Advancement of Science (AAAS). 1998. *Blueprints for Reform: Science, Mathematics, and Technology Education*. New York: Oxford University Press.

American Association for the Advancement of Science (AAAS). 2001. *Atlas of Science Literacy*. Washington, DC: AAAS; Arlington, VA: National Science Teachers Association. For the table of contents and sample "maps" from the *Atlas*, go to *http://www.project2061.org/tools/atlas/sample/toc.htm*.

Other AAAS Project 2061 documents are also available online. Begin your search at the Project 2061 home page: http://www.project2061.org/

National Research Council (NRC). 1996. *National Science Education Standards*. Washington, DC: National Academy Press. [available online at *http://search.nap.edu/readingroom/books/nses/*]

Nature of Science

"the" scientific method

The usual picture of "the" scientific method not only describes inaccurately how science works, but also distorts the meaning of words such as "theory" and "law." People often speak about the scientific method as if one, and only one, path exists toward scientific knowledge. If the scientist simply follows the scientific method scrupulously, according to the popular understanding of the term, he or she is certain to arrive at sure knowledge about how the natural world works. A commonly seen description for the scientific method describes a series of steps in which an observation leads to a hypothesis. Carefully tested, the hypothesis may become a theory and, if data continue to accumulate supporting the idea, may eventually be established as a scientific law.

No scientist follows a single set of four, five, or seven steps, in a certain order. In truth, you might say a scientific investigation begins with all the scientific work and knowledge the scientist brings to the lab. It is that knowledge, combined with observation (usually of something the scientist finds puzzling or at least interesting), that leads to the genesis of an investigation.

The resulting investigation may be experimental or observational. Scientists are often looking for relationships they think might exist between variables or testing predictions they would expect if an explanation they support was accurate.

Suffice it to say, biologists, geologists, and other scientists often follow radically different sorts of methods when they do investigations. Methods differ even within a scientific discipline. For example, a biologist studying an ecological system may need to spend days carefully observing an animal's behavior, trying to do nothing that would disturb the ecosystem. Alternatively, a molecular biologist working in a laboratory might set up an experimental situation that is very different from an organism's natural conditions; the biologist might grow a microorganism under special artificial conditions and then run it through a gel electrophoresis column.

Science is a process whereby new ideas are generated and put to the test. After testing, ideas are often discarded or modified—to be tested again. Sometimes ideas are modified in the middle of an investigation. Science is a human activity, and, as such, investigations and investigators don't follow a set of steps to be completed one after another. Scientists ask questions and probe nature looking for empirical evidence—data—to support their ideas and increase understanding. Ultimately, scientists make judgments about the validity of ideas. In some unofficial way, ideas are declared "true" when most scientists accept the evidence supporting an idea's truth.

inference (versus observation) An inference

is, basically, the result of logical reasoning. Science teachers, however, often distinguish between inferences and observations. An observation represents sensory input—information taken in directly through the eyes, ears, or other senses and through instruments that extend the senses, like infrared detectors. Inferences, in contrast, represent observations combined with the observer's prior knowledge or biases. Inferences are more subjective than observations.

Here's a classic example from high school science classes. It's more subjective to say, "I see a wax candle" than simply "I see a candle." After all, how do you know the candle contains wax, simply by seeing it from across a room? It could consist of something that looks waxy to you, but is actually plastic or some other material. Similarly, however, it's more subjective to say, "I see a candle" than "I see a cylindrically shaped object, white colored, with a length of approximately 10 cm."

Thus, it's more of an observation to say, "I see a cylindrically shaped object" than "I see a wax candle." "I see a wax candle" is an inference. There's no clear-cut point at which one statement can be declared an inference and a related statement an observation. It is probably possible, though, to declare a statement as being more inferential than another—more inferring is involved in some statements than others.

In reality, the distinction between an observation and an inference is ultimately arbitrary. Almost all observations are at least somewhat inferential. This is a point that philosophers of science noted more than a hundred years ago. Whether we call them observations or inferences, however, most science teachers ultimately have the same goal: to teach students to observe in ways that are as free from bias as possible.

induction, or inductive reasoning, is often discussed simultaneously with deduction. Together, they make up the two most common types of logical reasoning we use in science. They are also somewhat opposite to one another. Induction is the kind of thinking we use when we go from individual instances to a general conclusion, whereas deduction is the reverse—beginning with a general conclusion and going to individual instances.

Both ideas are much easier to understand with the help of examples. Suppose you are driving your car one day and hear a rattling noise, which goes away relatively quickly. A few days later you hear the noise again, and notice that both times the car was going 42 miles per hour. The next day, you again observe that the car rattles at 42 miles per hour—but that the car does *not* rattle at any other speeds. After a couple more days of the same observations, you logically conclude—using inductive reasoning—that your car rattles when it's going 42 miles per hour and at no other nearby speeds.

Reasoning inductively is something that's intuitive to almost everyone and has been extremely important in science. Almost all new scientific ideas began via someone's inductive generalization.

While induction is certainly logical, as well as important, readers should also understand that inductive reasoning certainly does not guarantee that the results will be correct in any sense of the word. If a student finds that he or she does particularly well on two or three tests when using a particular pencil, the student may inductively conclude a connection—and begin using his or her new "lucky" pencil exclusively! Indeed, not only good luck charms but also superstitions and stereotypes have often been born, ultimately, via a process of inductive reasoning.

Inductive reasoning is only a beginning in science. Inductively arrived at conclusions still must be empirically tested, evidence evaluated, and the ideas accepted by a preponderance of scientists before the ideas can be considered to be scientifically supported. Induction is not a foolproof way to generate new knowledge. Still, the creative act of inductive reasoning lies at the heart of new scientific ideas.

deduction is the kind of logical thinking we use when we start with a general premise and arrive at a particular, or specific, conclusion. "If ... and ... then ..." reasoning is usually deductive. For example, if all living things are made of cells, and a person is a living thing, then I would expect a person to be made of cells. This is deductive reasoning. Similarly, if earthquakes are caused by the movement of tectonic plates, and if I were to place devices to measure seismic movement throughout a continent, then I would expect to note more movement near plate boundaries than far from plate boundaries.

Deduction is the major way scientists test explanations—especially those involving abstract, or nontangible, concepts. Anything that can only be understood indirectly is tested deductively. The kinetic-molecular theory (all matter behaves as if made of invisibly tiny, constantly moving particles) provides a great example because it's so well established. Over the course of many generations, scientists have performed investigations with underlying thinking that I can generalize to the pattern "If the kinetic-molecular theory is accurate, and I [perform a particular investigation], then I would predict [the following results]."

As you think about it, you will recognize that a single deduction-based investigation supporting a conclusion certainly does not *prove* the conclusion to be true. If the kinetic-molecular theory is accurate, and an experimenter finds masses before and after a chemical reaction, she or he would predict the masses should not change. Finding that mass was conserved after several reactions, though, does not prove the kinetic-molecular theory.

Like induction, deduction is not a foolproof way to generate new knowledge. Decisions are ultimately made via the consensus of most scientists. Still, time has shown that inductive and deduc-tive reasoning—key to scientific methods—are the best ways we have to understand the observable world.

epistemology is the branch of philosophy that asks, How do we know what we know? Epistemology is concerned with figuring out whether we can trust that something is "true." In the case of science, that generally translates to mean "How do we know when we can accept a scientific conclusion?" and "What distinguishes conclusions considered inside versus outside the realm of science?" More than anything, scientific epistemology relies on empirical data.

Given that epistemological issues have been discussed for literally thousands of years, it is well beyond the scope of this small book to discuss the field with any depth whatsoever! I briefly mentioned epistemological problems with induction and deduction in the preceding entries. Classical arguments related to epistemology often also talk about the role of empirical information (sense data) versus rational or logical thinking; for example, what do we do when data don't seem to "make sense"? To what extent are our observations affected by our knowledge and the ways we think about the world—to what extent do people from different places, or different times, observe differently from one another? How much support is necessary before we can consider something to be "true"?

Data, for example, seem to support the idea that light is a wave—data from certain kinds of experiments are the kinds of data one would expect if light were a wave. Simultaneously, however, data from other experiments support the idea that light is made up of particles. It doesn't make logical sense to many people. Something can be a wave or a particle, but how can something be both at once? Nevertheless, empirical evidence supports this idea, and today we generally accept the idea that light acts as *both* a wave and a particle.

empirical, direct evidence, indirect evidence

When something is empirical, that means it is ultimately based on observation. Essentially, empirical information is what science people generally think of as data. If a conclusion is not empirically based, we generally don't think of it as scientific. The need for conclusions to be empirically based is probably *the* hallmark separating science from other ways of interpreting the world.

Empirical evidence supporting a conclusion can be *direct* or *indirect*. Direct evidence means pretty much what it sounds like—one directly observes something supporting a conclusion.

Indirect evidence is harder to explain. Indirect evidence is basically circumstan-tial evidence, although people sometimes think of that phrase as meaning lower quality evidence. Indirect evidence is powerful and important in science.

Virtually all evidence for anything that happened in the past is indirect, as is evidence for things tiny and, sometimes, far away. Since no one alive today actually saw George Washington, for example, all the evidence we have that a person named George Washington actually existed is indirect. Virtually everyone believes a person named George Washington existed; indirect evidence can be powerful and compelling. In fact, judges make life and death decisions in courtrooms everyday based on indirect evidence. If someone's fingerprint is found somewhere, we conclude (with a high probability) the person was there—even if no one saw him or her.

Likewise, people cannot "see" atoms with visible light—they're smaller than the light waves that would need to bounce off the atoms to make them visible! Still, we have abundant indirect evidence for their existence, and an entire branch of science—chemistry—is based on the conclusions that can be drawn when one assumes atoms exist. Similarly, no one was around to "see" dinosaurs and other things living on Earth millions of years ago, yet abundant indirect evidence supports the idea that plants and animals once lived on Earth, and, again, the entire science of paleontology is built on this conclusion.

variable Put succinctly, a variable is anything that varies! Experiments usually involve testing whether one thing that changes has a direct and predictable connection with another thing that changes. For example, a student scientist might be investigating whether varying the amount of fertilizer that plants get has a direct and predictable connection with plant growth. (The student would have to define what "plant growth" means; for our purposes, let's define plant growth as a plant's height.)

Researchers sometimes call the fertilizer the "independent variable" and plant growth the "dependent variable." In other words, if you suspect that one variable may cause another, the independent variable is the suspected causal agent and the dependent variable the suspected effect. The effect "depends" on the cause—hence the term "dependent variable." We also sometimes call the independent variable the "experimental variable," since it represents the variable the experimenter is consciously manipulating. Although the terms "independent variable" and "dependent variable" have distinct meanings, it's quite common for people to confuse these meanings. That's why I prefer terms like "experimental variable" or "suspected causal agent" and "outcome variable" or "suspected effect."

In setting up a good experiment, however, the experimenter must try to ensure that the only factor that might change the result—the dependent or outcome variable—is change in the experimental variable. In our plant example, that means the experimenter must try to create conditions where the only factor changing how tall the various plants grow is how much fertilizer he or she has applied to the plants.

Think about other factors that might affect plant growth—water, light, soil content. In a high-quality experiment, those variables would be kept the same from plant to plant. That way, the experimenter could attribute any differences in growth from one plant to the next to fertilizer differences alone. It's what children would call a "fair test." The experimenter purposefully tries to control, or keep constant, all the variables that might affect the experiment's outcome (the value of the dependent variable). These are usually called "controlled variables." The confidence we can have in the results of an experiment often depends heavily on how well the experimenter has controlled variables that might affect the experiment's outcome.

experimental designs (randomized, prospective, retrospective) Scientists
use various ways to test whether one variable causes, or is at least linked with, an-

other variable. (Things can be linked without one necessarily causing the other. Ashtrays are linked to lung cancer, but no one believes ashtrays cause lung cancer.) All good experimental designs, however, share the idea of trying to control conditions so that the only thing affecting values for the dependent variable (or outcome) are values for the independent variable. (See the previous entry for information on the word "variable.")

In the traditional *randomized* experimental procedure, the scientist tries to establish conditions whereby the independent or experimental variable is present in one (or more) experimental setups and lacking in the other setup. The setups are otherwise supposed to be identical. To use an example from the previous entry, testing whether fertilizer affects plant height, the scientist might create two identical fields located right next to each other. He or she would apply fertilizer to one field and not apply the fertilizer to the other field. Everything else would be the same. Thus, the scientist could attribute any differences in plant height to the fertilizer. (Note that the scientist could also create an experiment in which he or she created multiple identical fields, and each field received a different *amount* of fertilizer—including one field that received no fertilizer.)

A *prospective* experimental design is just like the randomized experimental design, except the scientist isn't the one applying the suspected causal agent (the fertilizer, for example). In this case, a prospective experiment would be one in which the scientist finds two (or more) fields that are identical, except that someone applied fertilizer to one field and no one has applied the fertilizer to the other field. Realistically, that does not happen often when people are doing experiments on things like plants. However, prospective designs are common in medicine and social sciences, where ethics, costs, or other factors make randomized experimental designs unrealistic.

For example, you might decide to use a prospective design when testing whether certain schoolwide discipline rules produce better student grades. It might be difficult for you to get schools you have chosen (because they are so similar) to employ or not employ certain schoolwide discipline rules, unless they were already planning on doing so.

In a prospectively designed experiment, you would find schools with and without certain schoolwide discipline rules. You would think of all the factors that might affect student grades (variables) and try to match schools in as many of these factors as you could. This is how scientists make prospective designs "fair." Having selected matching schools, you then proceed as you would with a randomized experimental design (monitoring what happens in the schools and doing anything you can to try controlling variables). Ultimately you determine student grades in the two schools. The more variables you can control, the more trust-worthy your results.

We call the third type of experimental design a *retrospective* design. In a retrospective study, the scientist begins with the *dependent* variable—the "results" or suspected effect. The scientist groups data into those that exhibit the suspected effect and those that don't. From here, the scientist looks for differences in values for the *independent* variable between the two experimental groups.

In the example we've been using, a *retrospective* study would be one in which the scientist looked for tall plants and short plants. If fertilizer helps plants grow, he or she would expect that farmers, let's say, had fertilized more of the tall plants than the short plants. Again, retrospective designs are rarely used with things like plants. Instead, they are used when ethics, cost, and time are important factors. Scientists can conduct retrospective studies more quickly than most other types of studies.

As an example, a scientist might use a retrospective study to determine whether there is evidence to support the idea that the presence of some chemical in drinking water gives people a particular digestive disease. The experimenter would look for people with and without the disease and then check whether or not the chemical is present in their drinking water. If the chemical causes the disease, the experimenter would expect to see a larger fraction of the sick people drinking water with the chemical than non-sick people.

Every effort is made to control variables in retrospective studies by carefully matching members of the two experimental groups (in this case, sick and non-sick people). However, in practice this can be difficult to do. Thus, retrospective studies are usually not conclusive. They do, however, provide for the possibility of useful data generated quickly, at less cost than other types of studies. (In a randomized experimental study, one would need to make one random group drink water with the chemical and another drink water lacking the chemical. The experimenter would monitor the people for many years, determining whether or not they got the stomach disease. This, of course, would be highly unethical, and, additionally, by the time researchers created conclusive data, many more people might have consumed the potentially toxic water.)

hypothesis Like the words

"theory" and "law," "hypothesis" is sometimes used differently by various people. The term has three commonly used meanings. First, some see a hypothesis as any tentative scientific conclusion—including both patterns or trends in data and explanations for observed patterns or trends. Some scientists use this as their definition of the term, as does almost everyone outside science.

Second, people examining the nature of science often use the term more narrowly, pointing to a hypothesis as being a tentative explanation or "explanatory hypothesis." Third, others see a hypothesis as being synonymous with prediction. This is the way students are often taught to use the word in preparing their science fair reports, for example.

To differentiate between the idea of a hypothesis as any tentative conclusion and a hypothesis as a tentative explanation, suppose that ten people take an experimental drug, and you notice that eight of the people start getting headaches. Although supported only by this small study, you tentatively conclude a link exists between the drug and headaches. Those who see a hypothesis as any tentative conclusion would describe this apparent link as being a hypothesis.

Those who describe hypotheses as being tentative explanations, however, would probably *not* see your current conclusion as being a hypothesis. If data continue to support the link between the drug and headaches, then your tentative *explanation* for why this link exists would be a hypothesis. (Perhaps you think the drug is constricting blood vessels in patients' heads, causing headaches, or maybe the drug causes headaches by making muscles in patients' necks and shoulders tense—causing tension headaches. Of course, it could also be that the headaches are connected to the disease the people were taking the drugs for in

the first place—the drug didn't cause the headaches, the disease did. Multiple explanations exist for the observed link.)

Either way, though, it's probably most important to understand this point: *A hypothesis is different from a prediction.* If a student is doing a science fair investigation to decide what type of paper towel is most absorbent, the student may *predict* that Brand X will hold the most liquid, but this is not a hypothesis. It's a prediction. In this case, the (explanatory) hypothesis might be something like "I think that thicker towels have more spaces to hold liquid." The student could then go on to say, "Because Brand X is the thickest towel we have, I predict it will hold the most liquid."

theory It may be that no term related to the nature of science is more misunderstood than "theory." The word has a very different meaning in science than it does in common usage outside science. To most people, a theory is a tentative scientific idea—something with more support than a hypothesis but not enough support to be considered widely accepted. This is what we mean when we say something is "only a theory" or "I've got a theory about that."

Although even scientists sometimes talk about theories this way, the term has a different meaning in science. A theory, in science, is a widely applicable explanation. Theories are well supported by data, but they are different from data or the generalizations that come from data (see "law" below).

Put another way, there is a major difference between a data *generalization* or pattern, and the *explanation* for the generalizations. A single generalization, in fact, may have multiple competing explanations.

An illustration or two will help readers understand the distinction. Consider all the generalizations that we've come to call "the gas laws"—Boyle's law, Charles's law, Guy-Lussac's law, and the general gas law. They represent four different generalizations, based on data. Chemists explain all these generalizations via the kinetic-molecular theory, which in fact stands at the heart of chemistry. It's the idea that everything behaves as if made of tiny, constantly moving particles. The theory beautifully explains the gas laws and any number of other phenomena (or generalizations).

Without acceptance of the kinetic-molecular theory, chemistry as we teach it wouldn't exist. However, people don't talk about this theory as being "just a theory." It's well established and important to the discipline of chemistry.

Similarly, the idea that living things have changed over time (evolution) and the theory that explains the generalization (natural selection) are at the heart of modern biology. Misunderstanding the idea of a scientific theory, though, leads people sometimes to think of evolution as "just a theory," as if the idea lacked empirical support and was highly tentative. In fact, evolution theory (like all good theories) is effective in explaining a wide range of phenomena.

To help your students understand that the word "theory" has such different meanings in and out of science, I suggest that you use the phrase "scientific theory" (rather than "theory"). Since students may already hold misconceptions about the concept of a theory, using this other phrase may help circumvent these preconceived ideas.

law In many ways, the idea of a scientific law is somewhat archaic today. Most of the laws we tell students about are more than a hundred years old—chemistry's gas laws, biology's genetics laws, Newton's physics laws, and Kepler's astronomy laws, for example.

Scientific laws, of course, still exist. It's just that we don't tend to think about the idea of absolute natural law anymore. Today we recognize scientific ideas as being tentative, and we realize that ideas (including laws) are subject to change and revision.

A law is a generalization or pattern people derive directly from data. If nature were a game, laws would be the rules. Laws don't magically come from data. They come when creative, knowledgeable people recognize something significant in the data before them. Generalizations, patterns, formulas, and even graphically displayed trends represent laws.

Readers should understand three key points about scientific laws, though. First, laws—like theories—are not usually based on a single (small) study. Established scientific laws, like theories, are well supported by data from multiple sources.

Still, that doesn't mean laws are eternal constants, never changing. All scientific knowledge, including laws, is tentative. Ptolemy's laws changed after Copernicus's and Galileo's work; physics laws of mechanics changed after Einstein's work; and developmental biology laws changed over time as well.

Second, laws are a different kind of knowledge than theories. Laws represent generalizations from data, and theories represent the ways we try to explain generalizations. Theories never become scientific laws, and laws were never theories. In the example from the "theory" entry above, Boyle's law and the other gas laws—all based on multiple experiments—are explained via the kinetic-molecular theory. The kinetic-molecular theory will never be called a law (just as the theory of natural selection, in biology, will never be called a law).

Third, laws are only valid for a specified range of conditions. For example, a law often explored in high school physics class is that the period of a pendulum (how long it takes to swing once) is independent of the size of the arc the pendulum is swinging through. The pendulum on a grandfather clock takes the same number of seconds per swing whether the clock is making "big" swings (soon after being wound) or "small" swings. This law, however, holds true only for a certain range of arc sizes—the law won't hold, for example, if the swings are "really big." Similarly, Boyle's law holds that a gas's pressure is inversely proportional to its volume—push on a gas and it will take up less space. The law holds, however, only under certain conditions (the mass and temperature of gas in the container are held constant, for example).

REFERENCES & FURTHER INFORMATION:

To learn more about experimental designs:

Carey, S. S. 1998. *A Beginner's Guide to Scientific Method*. Belmont, CA: Wadsworth.

To learn more about scientific methods and philosophical aspects of science:

Bauer, H. H. 1994. *Scientific Literacy and the Myth of the Scientific Method*. Urbana, IL: University of Illinois Press.

Derry, G. N. 1999. *What Science Is and How It Works*. Princeton, NJ: Princeton University Press.

Dunbar, R. 1995. *The Trouble with Science*. Cambridge, MA: Harvard University Press.

Wolpert, L. 1992. *The Unnatural Nature of Science*. Cambridge, MA: Harvard University Press.

INDEX

D

E

N

O

P

S